MY FEET HURT

Mike Harris

Published by New Generation Publishing in 2019

First Edition

www.newgeneration-publishing.com

INTRODUCTION

It's February 2011 and I am thinking about my forthcoming 50th birthday year, 2012, and what to do to celebrate the occasion. Priority 1: Alcohol. Priority 2: Umm more alcohol? Priority 3: Health; which to me means either playing five-a-side football or walking. Priority 4: Fun. Net result of these thoughts is a pub crawl - obvious really. Walking to a pub is an easily achievable goal and fulfils all of these priorities, whilst mixing drink and five-a-side football is a total disaster, so the choice was made!

Following this simple idea to celebrate, I then thought about combining it with something I'd always wanted to do and had been thinking about doing for ages, which was walking the whole of the Cornish Coastal footpath before I get too old and decrepit to cover the mileage. The walk, in my head, should therefore be from the Tamar Bridge all the way round (via Land's End) to Bude on the north coast - my home town - taking in the beauty of the place, enjoying the sunny weather, of course, oh and visiting a pub or two on the way – perfect!

After a quick e-mail exchange with my old school friend and occasional London-Bude drinking pal Chris Moore, which went along the lines of "This is spooky Mike, I was already planning the same thing for my 50th too!" we agreed that it was indeed a splendid idea and we would both work on a combined plan for the walk together. We both remembered slightly drunken vague conversation(s) where we'd established we both liked walking, beer (a lot), and the fantastic Cornish Coastline. We have a good friendship from our teenage years growing up in Bude too, and we were both heading towards 50 years old and needed to mark the occasion properly, so the rest is history as they say (whoever they are)!

Planning and organization over the next sixteen months resulted in “our event” that took place in the summer of 2013 and which we will recount for you now so you can see how we got along. There are many stories of the places we visited, some real characters and odd personalities we met, our friends who joined us on the walk or met us at various pubs along the way, and even a friend’s dog who made a guest appearance. In fact everything that makes a simple trip become a real adventure. Either way you can judge for yourself if it was fun; slightly or totally mad, enjoyable, physically and mentally testing and above all truly worthwhile.

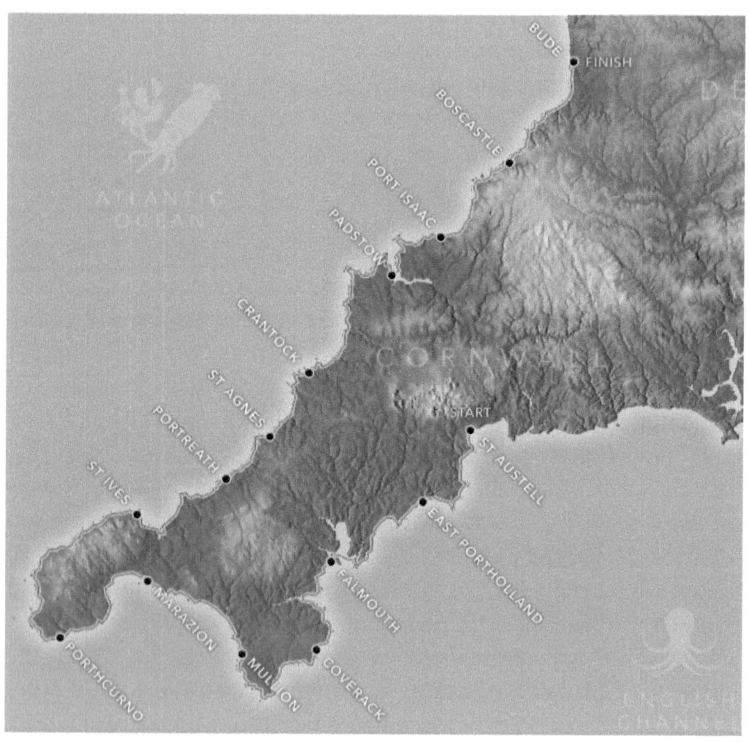

CHAPTER 1 – AND SO IT BEGINS

We now jump forward to the 29th June 2013, 7am, a cool, bright and clear Saturday morning and I am loaded up with my new rucksack (which will become my 'trusty' rucksack) holding everything I'd need for the next two weeks – I hope! I now cross the bridge at Paddington station, up from the London Underground and towards the Penzance mainline train that leaves in half an hour. My mobile beeps and there is a text message from Chris "And so it begins!" as he is on his way now from Virginia Water to meet me at Reading station, the first stop as we head towards St Austell in Cornwall for day one. Little does he know that I have already had disaster number one on my journey from my home in Harpenden to the local station, a portentous event and maybe a marker of things to come, but here's hoping I've got any bad luck out of the way already and the rest of the fortnight will be plain sailing.

As I was waiting much earlier that morning at Harpenden station and checking the train times into London St Pancras, everything was on time, great. So I put my hand in my pocket to check my mobile to see if there are any messages from Chris and then I realise that the mobile I have isn't mine – it was my wife's! Oh hell I think and then rummage around in my other pockets to find that I do in fact have my mobile as well, my wallet too, train ticket etc. so a feeling of total panic subsides slightly to just mere panic. Because of a phone company deal we'd ended up with the same type and coloured smart-phone, so I must have picked them both up off the kitchen table in my early morning excitement and last minute packing for the trip and am now thinking about what to do next. Do I just wait and post it back when I get a moment on the trip? Not really an option. Do I get a cab and head back home, except there are none around this early in the morning? Do I telephone the landline at home and wake everyone in the house? Will Shona be out walking the dog at this moment, oblivious to what's happened to her mobile and not be around? I decide to ring home and after five attempts she finally answers, sounding confused and a bit worried, not surprising having dropped me off less than ten minutes before! We sort out a quick plan and she drives to the station and picks up her mobile. Fortunately I had left plenty of time for last minute train cancellations, the experienced commuter speaking here, so as long as the tube didn't let me down I would be back on track for the Penzance train, phew. What a stressful start!

The Penzance train left on time and we met up as arranged at Reading and once settled we started to chat in earnest about the walk, comparing notes, accommodation plans, the guide book maps, ideas and checking with Chris's new exciting train app exactly where we were in the journey. Amazingly big signs outside on platforms stating places like Chippenham, Exeter St Davids, and Liskard were telling us where we were too, without the aid of Wi-Fi and the internet! Chris was undeterred though and enjoyed the exciting moment when his mobile was telling us were in Bodmin Parkway, one minute after we'd arrived in Bodmin Parkway! Fellow passengers in earshot may have been a bit annoyed with the app chat, but Chris's enthusiasm and excitement for the journey down was genuinely infectious and very much part of his character that he couldn't hold back. This enthusiasm never diminished, well not visibly or verbally to me throughout the fortnight, apart from one incident that we'll tell you about in chapter four. It shows how Chris's general attitude to life and merriment makes things great fun, even when we had some tough moments, especially from physical pain barriers and time pressures, throughout the walk and we will allude to these at the appropriate time in the story.

We'll now backtrack, as you may be wondering why we are going to St Austell and not the Tamar Bridge, the traditional gateway to Cornwall from the south, as we said in the introduction? St Austell is at least 25-30 miles west along the coast from there so are they cheating already I hear you ask? To explain this we need to look back at our planning stage when we soon realized that to cover the whole footpath we would really need at least two to three weeks, maybe more! We'd agreed with our respective families and work for two weeks away. Only fair to them and there is only so much everyone else is prepared to support and put up with as you head for your 50th birthday celebrations and are basically on a jolly away from everyone! It was also very easy to sit there and plan an 18 mile-a-day walk in the comfort of your home and/or office, not always so easy to actually walk it on the real coast-line! Indeed our optimism as to how many miles we could cover in a day was tested to the limit a few times, for me more than Chris, as you will see later on.

Anyway the upshot was we would start at St Austell as the train could take us there direct without any car worries. We also had a school friend who lived there too, Derek, known to us as the Mighty Tex but that's not part of our story - anyway he would meet us from the train and join in the walk for a few miles or even the whole day, depending on how he felt. Logistically, this was much simpler for us and a good way to get going without any car-dropping-off or picking-up hassle. At the other end of the plan as we had no car, we were going to leave our home town of Bude by local bus, catch the return train service to London from Exeter and get home this way on Sunday the 14th July after the two weeks away, all ready to head back to work on the Monday – easy!

Arriving at St Austell, not long after midday, we disembarked with our rucksacks in tow, very excited and glad that the travel app confirmed that we had actually arrived in St Austell, phew. We met Derek and his daughter Alice, the designated driver, for a short run to Charlestown on the southern side of the town. She soon got us to our first pit stop the appropriately named Wreckers Bistro to meet Caroline, Derek's wife, where we intended to grab a coffee and have a quick chat before we started on the planned trek to East Port-Holland via Mevagissey. Conveniently, the bistro was set on the quayside and Charlestown harbour road and at the edge of the harbour was the coastal footpath, our gateway for the long awaited (and very long) walk to Bude. Heading to the bar we were ordering coffees and cakes as food fuel etc. when Chris insisted on also starting with a beer too, impressive and fearless as is his way when it comes to beer. This was (and is, when the need arose) a lunchtime pick-me-up habit that would help sustain us going forward throughout the next two weeks as alcohol is fuel too, or so we kept telling ourselves; you can walk the effects off quickly as your body burns it up in the miles covered during our afternoon treks.

We arranged with Caroline and Alice that Derek would walk with us, resplendent in his brand new walking boots, as far as Pentewan and that we would have a late lunch there before they picked him up. So after all the planning, work and training we headed down to the harbour and joined the Coastal footpath to finally begin. Chris's philosophy was evident here as he rightly said that "As long as we keep the sea on our left hand side we must be going in the right direction", sound logic and meant we started off in the right direction, hooray!

CHAPTER 2 – EAST PORTHOLLAND

It really was good to finally get going and we were soon up and down the undulating coast heading passed Porthpean and getting used to the path, carrying the rucksacks and trying to set a decent pace as we had quite a way to go to East Portholland, our first overnight stop. These undulations I mentioned are a big feature of the Cornish coastal path if you've ever walked any of it and they were quite important for Derek because after each one he seemed to need to stop at the top, strike up a light and smoke his fag/tab/ciggie! This was to keep himself going he said, and to try to keep up with our pace as we were storming ahead in an excited, far too fast, not-got-the-steady-pace-yet speed. The day was already quite warm with the sun peeking through the early afternoon sky, so we found the initial going tough for all sorts of reasons; the increasing heat was noticeable but it was more due to the long grass of the (yet to be cut) path and very rugged field boundaries. If it was going to be like this for the rest of the walk we were in trouble, we thought, but nevertheless it was too late stop now and we ploughed on with our thoughts turning to liquid refreshment to counter the temperature and exertion through the grass. The three of us eventually got into the rhythm of chatting and walking, walking and chatting, stop for breath, allow Derek a smoke break, walking and chatting and before long we were heading downhill towards the Ship Inn, Pentewan, a great sight and our deserved late lunch stop.

At the pub we got an outside table and sorted the food. Indoors the friendly barmaid/manager tried to convince us to try the (then) relatively new Cornish lager "Korev". After the offer of a small taster glass Chris said "Yes great, is that a half to make sure we do like it then? Wonderful!" The barmaid/manager appreciated the joke and produced a couple of taster glasses for us and all was fine. What we weren't quite so aware of was the ABV level of the lager, which was 4.8%, meaning a slightly higher alcohol content than the more normal 3.8/4% etc. and this has a powerful effect (take note everyone, we want you all to drink sensibly – unless the occasion demands otherwise!). After a good lunch and some three pints later, we started up the hill a little merrily and began the trek towards the great port town of Mevagissey. Derek meantime had hoped to be picked up by Caroline and Alice after lunch and then meet up with us again later in Mevagissey Harbour, however the ladies had been enjoying their Saturday shopping, coffee etc. and informed him that they would meet us all in Mevagissey harbour later.

So the three of us were still together after-all and the steady pace soon re-emerged, though Derek was feeling a bit grumpy at this stage as his new boots were really starting to hurt, he'd walked farther than intended and had "Korev" lager pumping around his system on the cliff tops. He was not the only one being affected by the heat and alcohol. As we descended a dry, stony part of the path, Chris slipped forwards and due to the weight of his rucksack over-balanced and fell on his knees with loud crash. I was directly behind him and Derek was behind me and it looked bad. Chris dusted himself down after we'd helped him up, but then grimaced with each step - as he moved forward, each time his ankle went down I heard a click, and thought "Hell, that's it we're three hours into the walk and it's all over, Chris has broken his ankle or snapped something, shit!" He then announced it was fine, his cut knee hurt but no worries, so let's crack on when Derek finishes his fag. The clicking I heard was not Chris's ankle at all but Derek's cigarette lighter behind me as he'd clicked his lighter in perfect timing to Chris's foot movement, phew. I was mightily relieved and we all cracked up laughing realising what had gone on, so after Derek finished his fag and Chris had sorted his wound out, off we went to Mevagissey.

The sun was shining and the sky was azure blue as we arrived in the harbour and found the town completely swamped with people out enjoying themselves - what was going on? Turned out it was the Mevagissey and South Cornwall carnival day and we'd arrived into the middle of a street party, brilliant fun! Now Derek had been promising us great Cornish ice-creams once we got to the town, in which of course I indulged, missing this real taste as it never is quite the same in London or elsewhere. However, Derek went and bought something else entirely at the parlour! Was there something I didn't know? What was he doing? Anyway Chris (as will be a recurring theme in the walk) swapped a quick sugar rush now for a potential pint later. We then sat in the sun on the harbour wall and considered a new plan as it was already late afternoon and Chris and I still had to get to East Portholland, which was at least 8 to 10 miles away. The B&B we'd booked was another 2 miles in-land from the footpath and time was fast running out for us to get there by any sensible time. What were we to do? We always thought day one was going to be the toughest in terms of distance versus time in our plan so the thinking caps were on.

Caroline and Alice had now joined us after struggling to park the car in the town with the festival going on, and we came up with a tactical masterpiece. They could drive us ten minutes further along the coast to re-join the footpath, we'd miss out the Penare headland thus saving us about two hours walking, leaving us maybe 4 miles or so to walk from Hemmick Beach to East Portholland. In the meantime we now had time to buy our drivers a well-deserved drink (non-alcoholic of course) in the appropriately named Harbour Tavern, which was located conveniently on the harbour wharf. Chris, Derek and I continued with a pint and we were thinking at this point we had probably drunk as many pints as miles covered, not a great idea for the forthcoming 200-220 miles ahead. But it's not often we get to meet our old friends in Cornwall and it was a great atmosphere in the town, so we thought why not indeed. Also we were starting to realise that though beer is a food with calories galore, the constant walking burns the alcohol up much quicker than you think so a good tip everyone, start walking a lot!

By now we had also realized that though our plan was good on paper, we would have to be prepared to continually adjust it depending on whom we were walking with, how good the path was, the mileage and where we needed to get to that day, how the feet and legs were coping, was our stamina good enough, could we read the map and guide book properly, did the sign post accurately reflect the terrain, and was the pub too good to leave? The only thing in the end we didn't really have to worry about was the weather. Only once did it rain for half a day and for the rest it was always dry, even if cloudy sometimes, and as the walk progressed a fantastic blocking high pressure weather system from the Azores came in and kept us dry and sunny for nearly the whole time. We felt very lucky as there are few places better or more beautiful in the world than the Cornish coast on a sunny, clear and warm day and our timing turned out to be near perfect. Walking in the rain is fine for a day or two and this is the price you pay sometimes for getting out into the countryside and meeting the elements of nature first hand, but not for two weeks solid thank you very much.

So the intrepid walkers were still in the Harbour Tavern enjoying the company and general good atmosphere that is Mevagissey in festival mood and progress had been slower than planned. Finally the time had come for us to return to the footpath and do some walking (about time too I hear you say). We had a merry car journey down to Hemmick Beach which according to Caroline's recollection was three men giggling and laughing in the back of the car all the way there. After much gratitude for the help and company on our first day we waved goodbye to the Barr family and headed up the coast towards East Portholland and our first overnight stop. As we set off the evening sky was just turning light yellow and orange and would become red with the changing sun as it began its descent towards the horizon. We hoped we had time to get to our destination before darkness descended as this was June. It was also the first time the two of us were alone on the footpath without Derek, apart from the sheep and other wildlife, and it all was all suddenly very real from the days of planning in our minds, on paper and in the digital world.

We followed Chris's maxim of "Keep the sea on our left and we can't go wrong" and he was designated the lookout and I was designated map and guidebook reader. This was due to his long sightedness for the further away land marks and path ahead, whilst my short sightedness would be best for all the text reading and map checking close up work. A perfect combination to make up for our eyes not being 20:20 but then we were fifty years old and these things do have a habit of catching up with you. This combination worked well on many an occasion. I would describe where we should be heading to and what should be there, Chris would spot them in the distance and on we went. Our only real problem was that we were in fact using the map and guidebook upside down and backwards! I will hastily explain that we are not totally mad; just that in the excellent guidebook that we agreed to use, the travellers had gone from Bude to Plymouth, whilst we were heading the other way. So both of us had fun all fortnight reading the map and processing the text the other way around from how it was written, but all necessary as the guide was very detailed, described exactly what we were doing, the maps were clear and the information contained in it was 95% up to date at the time we did it. The 5% error was down to ferry times and a lot of stress will be revealed at the river crossings later because of it.

As we arrived in Port Holland, the East-West name split is basic logic from which side of the river you are on, and we knew we needed to go inland from the coast but we didn't know where our B&B was exactly or where Tubbs Mill was, where it took its name from. Our guidebook and map didn't cover the inland areas, so to keep our paperwork carry to a minimum (for weight and hassle purposes) we were going to ring any difficult to find places once when we arrived at a sensible point on the route. However, thanks to the communication infrastructure of Cornwall, we had no phone signal at all to contact the B&B, great. We wanted to let them know we were at the beach and aiming to arrive as soon as we could, hopefully by 9pm, could they hold some food and could they tell us exactly how to get there, you know the sort of thing needed at this point? This was a feature of all our trips where we were up against the clock as these simple requirements make life and the walk go more smoothly, plus it helped us from not having to sleep in a hedge and wake up next morning in the rain, starving etc.

So not being afraid of minor challenges we thought we'd actually talk to some locals to get directions by human conversation and not the internet, because we simply didn't have access to it. Now where were the locals? It suddenly dawned on us that it was a very small hamlet and there was no one in sight, at all. No cars moving, not even a dog barking, or a cat sunning itself, there didn't seem to be any insects buzzing around either - there was no sign of life anywhere. We were beginning to wonder if the town had been hit earlier in the day by a neutron bomb and killed every living thing in it and that we'd walked into some terrible horror show! Chris then spotted a red telephone box, thank goodness and we headed over to make a landline call to the B&B - how very analogue and retro, cool. Inside however, it was not good as looking down, we noticed two plants growing in the corner, the money box didn't work when I tried to put a ten pence piece in and there was no dial tone - it was basically knackered and so were we.

Right, there was only one thing to do, we would have to find a house with someone still alive and ask for directions so off we went down the right hand side of the river where most of the houses were. All of them seemed empty, locked up, no-one home until we got to the end cottage where a window was wide open and there were sounds of life via a TV and voices. The friendly local stuck his head out as we approached and told us (in a generic South East England accent!) where the B&B was, so after thanking him, off we trekked into the wilds of Caerhays to find our accommodation. It took us about an hour to walk along the high-hedged lanes and crossroads but we found it and the landlady was very welcoming, and the place itself (a converted mill) was very impressive too. It was a great relief to have finally made it and we sat down to our quick salad meal, which was all they could do at that late hour, meeting the husband who sorted out the food. It turned out to be a very expensive salad, which Chris still grumbles about to this day, but needs must as I always say! Anyway we got settled for the night and the accommodation standard was very high; just what we needed at the end of a very long and eventful day. Both our thoughts and chat was about how sometimes you can cram an amazing amount into twenty four hours if you just go for it. Day one was over and we had survived. To think that earlier in the morning we were both at our respective homes in South East England and now, late at night, here we were in the middle of South Cornwall and the prospect of a very long and adventurous walk to Bude in front of us. Not a bad way to mark turning fifty.

CHAPTER 3 - FALMOUTH

The following morning, Sunday the 30th June 2013, we were up bright and early and started on our new (and fun to us!) routine of re-packing the rucksacks and sorting out our gear for the day. This was to become a well-organized routine that took less and less time as our efficiency increased, in fact it became quite therapeutic as the fortnight went on. Needless to say as this was only day two and our first attempt at the re-packing, something was missed and Chris ended up leaving his light fleece behind, but we decided this was a good omen for the weather because it will be warm and we won't need it anyway. Why didn't you go back and get it once you'd found out it was missing, or at least contact the B&B to get them to post it home I hear you ask? Well let me explain.

The landlady as we said was very friendly and helpful but, had insisted the night before as we sat and ate, without any prompting from the tired duo, to tell us her and her husband's life story, travelling around India on her own, he was a builder, how they ended up in Cornwall etc. Not really what we needed after a tiring day. As we started breakfast the following day we had the same treatment of "I'll leave you to your breakfast" and then she promptly sat down and chatted about all the problems of re-building the Mill, issues around the local area, that sort of thing. The previous night was fine from a polite we were guests' point of view, but now we needed to check our plan for the day and work out timing and logistics for the 20 miles to Falmouth including a ferry we had to catch to avoid a 10 mile detour that we could not afford to do. We just needed some time to ourselves. However, the discussion with her meant we ended up getting the offer of a lift back to the coastal path as her husband was driving that way, so we were grateful with an hour of walking back down the lanes being saved. I also nearly left my wallet behind on the desk after sorting out the bill and that would have been disaster number two if she hadn't spotted it, so I was in her debt! Anyway after saying our goodbyes and wondering if all the landladies and landlords we were going to meet would be like this (some definitely were!) we loaded up the car and drove off. The husband dropped us right at the beach road where we'd left the night before and once back on the footpath we were on our way to Falmouth.

The morning weather was a bit cool and cloudy with a hint of rain so we had our macs ready and this is when Chris discovered his fleece was missing but decided we didn't have time to go back. He would also not contact the B&B either - it could well have been a very long conversation and a lot of hassle for a £15-30 light fleece that we agreed wasn't needed due to the guaranteed hot weather we would have. This, at the time, was pure hope but turned out to be a good omen for the fine weather that arrived a bit later in the week and never left us. As we climbed the first cliff there was no-one in sight; before us and to our left the grey sea and sky spread out to the south and west, the green- brown path was ahead and we were bound for the first town en-route which was Portloe.

Now we were getting into our stride and pace of carrying the rucksacks as well as getting used to the terrain and path. Here it was pretty good and we were soon at Portloe, a lovely inlet harbour with steep sides to the path into and out of. We afforded ourselves a small water stop and map check once we'd reached the top of the hill out of the port, and looking back it seemed a long way already. We were under a bit of time pressure as according to our guidebook, the ferry crossing to Falmouth would close by 6pm, so we had to get our skates on. The 20 miles was one of the longer days we'd planned and we had no idea how variable the walk could be, what mileage would be sensible, how the legs and feet would cope on day two? This was a big learning curve for us but all part of the challenge, good fun and a really good way to get fit. It took time for us to adapt to the conditions and what was needed were visual reference points to aim at, maybe it is just a human thing relying on our vision so much, but this is what we did as we strode across South Cornwall and the English Channel side of the Peninsula.

The first visual reference was Gull Rock, a Prometheus type outcrop in the sea off the Nare headland, which we could see from East Portholland and which seemed to grow in size and shape as we made our way down the coast. It was a good target and as it slowly got bigger we knew we were making progress. The second was an enormous tanker just out to sea beyond the headland, but obviously anchored to head into the deep water port of Falmouth at some point. Chris pointed out that this was his beer supply ship that had been commissioned to land ahead of our arrival and started jokes about how St Austell brewery shares had doubled since our walk was announced, how Sharpe's 'Doom Bar' production was doubled, that sort of thing. The weather meantime was slowly getting warmer and we'd already got rid of our macs as the sun made a brave attempt to shine through the cloud breaks.

At this point we were thinking about a decision which, due to the ferry time constraints, we'd have to make: do we head across land (even via roads) to cut off the headland at St Anthony on one side of the river, going down the other side via the coastal path to St Mawes and catch the ferry to Falmouth from there? Or would we risk the long headland walk to St Anthony and take the ferry from there to St Mawes and then onto Falmouth? We decided we'd ask at the locals at the planned lunchtime pit stop in Portscatho and get some expert advice as to what we should do - this was our compromise.

With the sun just about breaking through and the temperatures rising we now headed downhill into Portscatho and I was trying to work out from the guide where the pub Plume of Feathers was. It was here that I first saw Chris and his pub-time speed walk rate, which was a sudden and massive increase and unstoppable. We couldn't see the pub and being under time pressure there was a bit of panic creeping in so Chris sped off into distance whilst I was consulting the map and tried to keep up. An unsuspecting local was set upon by Chris in his firmest voice demanding to know where the pub was, to which the visual reply was basically shaking and pointing to the next road and mumbling "It's that way" such was the force of Chris's body language and speed of approach! I joke and exaggerate of course, he wasn't really that bad, just to the point, as we did need food and drink and had to get on.

Fortunately, for the rest of the locals, we immediately found the pub and sorted out lunch and drinks and got advice from the bar staff about our predicament along the lines of "We are not sure really?" which was fair enough I suppose. Doing this walk we realised, at times like this, how people spend so much time travelling around by car and don't know much of the local landscape on the coastal path beyond the beach car park and the headlands either side. As we ate our lunch we decided to use the roads and cross by land to St Just and then head down the footpath to St Mawes as we couldn't possibly miss the crossing - not ideal as the aim was to enjoy the beauty of the sea views and coast, not walk along country roads, however peaceful.

With a bit of map reading and guess work we at least worked out a public footpath route which meant we only had to walk a little bit along a C road and for a small part of the A3078 (in fact just one hill) and cross two fields before we got to St Just, what could possibly go wrong? The first thing was to find the public footpath, which we did, and so left the road and crossed into a lane and all was well. At the triangle junction with farms and houses and other dwellings leading off in all directions, however, there was no public footpath sign in sight, we went up and down a few times before finding the right road; it was now sunny and we were getting annoyed at the wasted time. Off we went and then there was the second field and a broken sign to follow, which was a relief. Into the field we went and the path should have been straight across according to our map, but instead all we could see was a ploughed field with massive furrows and hard dry soil since the farmer had clearly just ploughed across the whole thing obliterating the footpath in the middle, typical! Well we'll go around the side then and it must continue over there amongst the trees and hedges on the far side. Could we find it? No, and now we really were worried. If you remember the un-cut grass and field boundary comments from chapter one, well this was June and everything was at maximum leaf and height and growth and the same! We were determined not to head back to the road unless absolutely the last resort. Fortunately Chris's long sight managed to pick up a wooden signpost across a tiny gap in the overgrown hedge-row so we fought our way through the jungle to re-join the path down to Trethem Mill and… we were back on track, phew! This was a good lesson for us and we determined never go inland or leave the coastal footpath, and we would stick to that doctrine all the way, apart from the times we didn't!

At St Just we followed the road and directions to the coastal path and as we crossed one of the small squares we noticed a Kings Ferry timetable sign announcing the ferries at this time of the year ran until 9.30pm, oh how we laughed! All that stress, and missing out on the St Anthony peninsula walk for roads and jungle! Still it meant we could now relax, ease the pace of the walk down the coastal path to the impressive St Mawes castle, and look forward to our night out in Falmouth. It clouded over and was cooling off again as we arrived at the crossing point and embarked onto the ferry for the twenty minute journey to the central Quay. We were in good spirits despite the now grey sky, grey water, looming dockyards of the deep-water port and darkening skies. It was the first time I'd ever been to Falmouth so we sat down on the ferry and started planning where to eat once we'd found the B&B, what beers we could drink and whether we should choose one as our un-official walk beer?

The crossing was calm as we headed to the other side of the bay with Pendennis Castle on our left provided a historical backdrop to the modern buildings all around. We disembarked, got our bearings with the map, me reading, Chris checking the land marks, street names and pubs (of which there seemed a few!) and then we headed off to find the Braemar Guest House. It was only a short walk up the hill and we got settled in very easily as this was a clean, efficient place, and our room was fine. We then needed to get food etc. so we retraced our steps back to the harbour and entered the Quayside pub for a simple meal and a few beers.

The young barman serving us told us there was some meal-deal with beer etc. for a fair price so we thought bargain, we'll do that. Chris then came up with the idea of having the biggest one we could possibly be served with on the menu and a food race to see who could actually finish it. After thirty minutes of chomping, another beer and general chat Chris easily finished first and enjoyed the victory moment, whilst I had finally given up! We then turned to important matters of contact with home and the outside world as we'd received lots of texts and messages wishing us well and trying to find out where we were. Before we left, I had had the great idea of setting up a Facebook page for just this purpose, meaning we could do everything like send and receive messages and upload photos of our travels, the perfect use of modern technology by two ageing gents. We had a problem though, I knew how to use Facebook on a PC, tablets being new, very expensive, quite bulky and not really practical on this type of trip and Chris knew how to use his iPhone. The simple fact was I didn't know how to use an iPhone, but was on Facebook. Chris was not on Facebook and had no idea how it worked, but he knew how to use an iPhone, so it emerged that we were in fact two old blokes who couldn't use the modern technology available for the time being. So our solution to the problem was let's have another beer and think about it - which we did.

Feeling a bit tired we at least managed to text everyone we really needed to and thought it was time to head back up the road to our B&B to get ready for the next morning. Falmouth seemed to be quite busy and friendly with lots of bars, people, cars and Sunday night revellers and it was a pleasant walk back up the hill and Avenue Road. Once inside the comfortable and functional room we both tried to sort out the phone and get at least a picture of our adventures uploaded, and so began the inevitable modern struggle with local WI-FI, passwords, network ID, battery power, signal strength, space radiation, weather interference, bat nests and all the other hassle that really should be sorted out with a simple standard National WI-FI system we all pay for collectively so that we all can use everywhere at all times, instead of the fragmented chaos of private communication networks, grrr… but that's another topic. Anyway rant over and back to the intrepid fifty year old technological luddites as we managed to upload a picture to the Facebook page – hooray! Not being trained or used to blogging on-line (or on-phone, on-pad) and telling the whole world everything as it happens constantly from what you have eaten to every mundane human thought/process/ idea/event etc. we didn't actually manage to write anything. Something useful like where we were and how many miles we'd done already would have been a good start, but we were novices and would get better as the days went by. Well, quite a few days would go by and we continued to struggle as you will find out as we needed to make friends with an eighteen year old techie, learn to wait until after 10-30pm when guests had gone home/to bed so the WI-FI got quicker and other tricks of the trade.

CHAPTER 4 - COVERACK

We woke up to a bright sunny Monday morning on the 1st July 2013, all refreshed after a quick breakfast, both of us getting more efficient at packing our rucksacks and not leaving anything behind in the Guest House. This had already become a vital daily routine and also became very therapeutic over the walk as it really sets the mind to the task ahead for each day once the bags were packed. Which today was to head to the lovely village of Coverack where we would meet Chris's sister Tess and their family friend Jacky who were going to walk with us for a few days. So we bid our farewell to Falmouth and headed down the hill to the Gylly beach café end of Gyllyngvase beach where we would pick up the Coastal path once more. There was however a slight problem for me as my left foot was killing me, as I think the first of many blisters was already starting. My initial thought was that I can't do this, my feet are dying and we're only on day three, what am I going to say to Chris? He was his usual chipper self and we decided to get to the beach, sit down and plan the route carefully as we had (as the song says) two rivers to cross today. Geographical diversion, the South Cornish coast is much more river estuaries, green and lush vegetation, and small cliffs on the English Channel. The opposite of the Lizard and Land's End Peninsula's and our beloved massive cliffs and sandy beaches of the Atlantic North coast. However, we both really enjoyed the different atmosphere down here as neither of us had experienced it before and it was all part of the feeling of adventuring into the unknown.

Back to the injured foot and for whatever reason, the tight feeling seem to subside and the pain eased dramatically as we walked along, so I decided to say nothing and just keep going as we headed along the beach and coastal path. Our aim was to get to the Helford river crossing and either grab an early lunch there depending on crossing times, or plough on to the hamlet of Porthallow after we'd got over the Gillan creek crossing, which was the other side of Helford, thereby avoiding an impossible 10-15 mile hike around the road way. The fields and cliffs seem to just whizz by and we had some great views of Falmouth bay as the sun continued to shine and we made good progress to Helford passage beach where we picked up an important Cornish ice-cream and the Ferry Boat over to the village itself. A lovely little crossing in calm easy waters and we hitched up on the other side of the river in no time heading for Gillan creek. As we went along to the village we stumbled across (Chris's laser beer vision spotted) the Shipwright Arms, which looked very inviting for a beer and an early snack, so in we went. It was here we decided, well Chris had come up with the idea in Falmouth which I endorsed fully, that our un-official walk beer was going to be St Miguel lager that we were happily slurping. Looking back with hindsight we should have had Tribute as our un-official ale beer as well as the lager, but the weather was generally so good that a cool lager seemed to fit and only once did I revert to my ale (on the only day it actually rained in the whole of our two week adventure!)

Fully refreshed we walked around a wooded headland to Gillan creek where we joined up with a few other intrepid walkers and tourists who were awaiting the small boat to cross the creek from the wooden pontoon/jetty sticking out in the sun. Once over the creek we went back up to the cliffs once more and onto our next stop, Porthallow and hopefully lunch. Porthallow, a name that will be synonymous to us for the unhelpful miserable side of the Cornish character and its love-hate relationship with tourists and tourism that goes on every summer. Chris refuses to mention the name now and has tried hard to blot it out of his memory, even though it's actually a nice place, anyway let me explain why this was the case…

After another hour or so of a pleasant stroll I was looking at the map and guidebook and time seemed to be getting on so we both agreed to quicken the pace as we headed downhill towards the cove. In the distance was a pub and we thought that'll be a fine place to stop. At the same time along the path were a couple walking their dog, which happened to be a

Border Terrier, the same breed as my dog Whiskie, so I started chatting to them as dog owners do and Chris's beer scope was eyeing the pub when the woman mentioned that the current Landlord doesn't always have the pub open during week days – WHAT! Chris's beer antennae and speed walking mode immediately kicked in and he was off like a rocket, making his usual comment to me of he'll order the beers whilst I sort the map and money out when I get there, see you in a bit. Off he went at a tremendous pace and the couple with me were hopeful that the pub would be open for a change as it was July and a beautiful sunny day and he would therefore have four hungry and thirsty customers to serve already. As I tracked Chris's progress I looked over to the pub and spotted on the large red/burgundy door (which was obviously shut) a square white piece of paper or sign pinned to it - always a bad sign. This did not bode well as we all made progress down the path and another couple were at the pub with bags and cases looking a bit lost, meanwhile Chris had finally got there and was obviously annoyed, harrumphing around up and down the road giving the Five Pilchards Inn a very hard stare. As we all finally made it to the road outside another few tourists on the beach seem to morph along with the now happy throng of eleven potential paying customers and at last a builders/electrician/ decorator/ handyman type van turned up and out popped the Landlord/ Owner/Tenant/Man in charge. Great we all thought, he was just late and the pub would be open soon, how wrong we all were. He was only here to let the two guests with cases in to the guest house bit and their rooms, no he wasn't going to open the pub not even for drinks and definitely not for food and that was final. He didn't really want to run the pub but had to due to his family something or other and he really didn't care about the potential custom. This to me and Chris was the other side of the Cornish character where it was obvious this was not his main job, something he wasn't interested in and tourists were a nuisance that just had to be endured until they all went home. We were used to it growing up with a few local people feeling the same way about the tourists and industry that didn't always directly benefit them, and on one level you can't blame them really, but…!

So what to do next? I diplomatically waited quite a while and suggested we get some food from the village shop, which we did, and then joked we could get a rum and raisin ice-cream too? Not quite a nice pint of ale or lager and Chris fumed, smiled and saw the funny side too as we sat out on what was actually quite a nice beach for our improvised non-alcoholic lunch. After half an hour's sit-down a runaway puppy from nowhere charged over towards us with an anxious owner running behind and all Chris needed now was this bundle of energy and fur to either steal his food or pee on his bag and this eventful day would have been totally complete. Fortunately it was just being friendly and we soon had it back under control and returned to its thankful owner, so we got up and found the footpath at the end of the beach and were on our way once more for the last walk of the day to Coverack.

The weather remained warm and we went past the massive Porthoustock quarry and harbour wall, part of an industrial landscape we knew nothing about, that still quarries for road materials etc. It was quite impressive with its big stone mill and general open cast rock mining equipment. As we passed Godrevy cove further along, we came to an older looking concrete jetty sticking out to sea one way and some old massive iron and steel structures inland with more quarried rock towering over us the other way. What on earth was this place? We bet none of this was in the tourist brochures but they had a raw working quality, massive rocks and a dis-used air about it that made it a memorable place to see. Apparently it had been used for stone quarrying from the late 19th Century and was used in world war two to provide stone for Cornwall's airfields as well as the other present day uses. This was part of our idea for the walk, to see things we'd never come across despite growing up in the county and you never know what is around the corner once you are out and about.

We continued along a long, physically tough part of the coastal path that was testing my foot once more as the pain returned. I found it really hard because it seemed that we were walking along scrubland with rocks everywhere and not on a defined path, but Chris seemed not to be phased and we trekked on until the sight of the lovely curved bay of Coverack came into view and down the hill we went into the village. Now we just needed to find Penmarth House where we were booked in for the night and would also meet up with our next guest walkers who would join us for two full days walking. Chris looked at the tourist notice board for information and I spotted a local who was bound to know and politely asked where it was, to which he replied politely with an accent, that he was a German tourist and had no idea. Fortunately we could see up the hill a big stone clad house that looked right and the directions on the town notice board seemed to point to this building, so up we went.

Upon arrival we met the landlady who seemed a bit eccentric (oh no not another one!) and the place had a rambling feel to it as we were shown around. Outside there were plant pots, equipment and hosepipes all over the garden and drive, whilst inside there were boxes of stuff everywhere, the kitchen looking quite cluttered (but then real working kitchens often do) and finally two piles of pictures that need to be sorted on either side of a balcony as we went upstairs. The place itself was huge and the views and the southern light filtering into the place made it quite impressive but we had this feeling that we were an inconvenience as guests, and both of us were trying desperately hard not to giggle behind the lady's back. So we'd found another B&B with an unusual owner and would this theme continue we wondered? When we were shown to our rooms, which were absolutely fine by the way, the landlady mumbled something about her going for an operation the following day, but that her husband would sort breakfast and that we'd find everything we needed in the room with a throwaway comment about a kettle and general muttering and mumbling as she went back downstairs. We found the kettle on the floor!

Chris now seemed to go into anxious mode as his older sister Tess and their family friend Jacky were due to arrive and they were staying in the other wing of the house and he was feeling the responsibility of other people joining the walk quite keenly. Meanwhile I set about repairing some of the damage to my foot with blister packs and plasters and getting ready for the evening and meeting the new walkers. We had the same problem of lack of WI-FI, no phone signal etc. and we both tried texting to no avail as the poor communication of modern smartphone technology with no network coverage was very apparent so I decided to use the landline technology of a phone box that could give me a clear line instantly to anywhere in the world if we found one. As to our Facebook page and blog, it was hopeless.

We all met up downstairs, went through introductions for me and my vague memories of Tess back when I was sixteen to eighteen years old and an occasional visitor to Chris's house and Jacky who seemed to know my older brother Pete from school days. A friendly start anyway and we headed off down the hill chatting about how odd the couple were that ran the guest house, but we all had reasonable rooms and were hoping that the promised free range eggs/home grown tomatoes type breakfast would be fine, despite the strange atmosphere about the place. We went to the Paris Hotel restaurant for our evening meal, opposite the old lifeboat station at the end of the cove. It was a lovely sunny evening and Chris was in a much happier mood now he'd met up with Tess, got some alcohol in front of him and fun company to get over some of the day's events. On the way down I'd also managed to make my landline call home from the said telephone box, which at least worked this time unlike the one in East Portholland and managed to speak to my wife and relay some of what we'd done and that I was still alive etc. Thank goodness we had some alternative to mobile communication failures down here. The meal chat was a plan for the next morning and where we'd meet up for breakfast once Jacky had sorted out where her car would be parked for their return trip when they would leave us, and we would all start bright and early for the walk to Mullion.

Chapter 5 – Mullion

Despite our trepidations from the night before the breakfast from the host was excellent and he was quite funny and generally charming/mad with his conversation and attitude to us and obviously worried about his wife's impending operation. So afterwards we bade farewell to another eccentric landlord and put our best feet forward and headed off back to the beach and footpath. With the four of us now we had to adjust to the different pace and general chit chat that goes with a bigger party but we soon got into the walking rhythm and the atmosphere was one of fun, chat and the enjoyment of the adventure ahead of us all.

The weather however seemed, for the first time, not to be on our side and of course we felt sorry for Jacky and Tess as we'd been boring them with tales of the fantastic walking weather the previous evening. For all of us it was the wet weather gear out. Chris and I had planned not to keep going by foot for more than two days if the rain kept coming. With the right company in the rain it can be (and was fun) but you pay a price in terms of your feet, clothing and general cold of that seeps into you after a prolonged exposure - as I found out by the end of this the toughest day (for me) of the whole trip. We were prepared to use public transport if necessary and we'd make use of and enjoy all the boat crossings too, since we would have needed double the time without them.

We were now on the Lizard Peninsula which is the most southern tip of Cornwall and a place I'd always wanted to visit. The terrain we were on was quite tough and testing in the cloud and light drizzle rain that blew over us in waves and pulses, but didn't diminish our jokes and conversation as we passed through Lankidden Cove, taking in the impressive rocks and cliffs that announced we were no longer in the river estuaries, wooded promontories and almost tropical plant life of the Channel side and were heading for the Atlantic ocean, which always feels like home to me. Having seen it on my past travels in Portugal and South Africa, the fresh air, wave structure, even the colour of the sea seemed the same as off Cornwall, despite the massive distances away from each other on the earth. Maybe funny or odd (is it me?) but that's how I feel about the Atlantic and having the privilege of growing up beside the ocean makes you realize what a beautiful place the sea is, most of the time. Massive amounts of water everywhere that unfortunately seemed to be pelting down on us all of a sudden, just to wake me out of my nostalgic mind wanderings.

As we headed across Kennack Sands we'd agreed to meet more friends Jonny and Jane Martyn who were on their holidays down here and who we'd all be meeting back up with in Bridgerule, near Bude for their wedding at Jonny's farm on the final Saturday of our trip. So it seemed a great idea for them to join us for a day's walking. We'd agreed to meet them at the Kennack Sands beach café and it all went to plan with us all grabbing a coffee and tea as we met up. Jane asked keenly how we'd found the walk this morning and did we see her message to us written in the sandy beach? Message, what message we all said? Sadly we'd changed tack and gone around the big gap in the rocks on the upper part of the beach and on to the café and had completely missed her message welcoming us, written with stones neatly on the lower part of the beach, such is the problem of an improvised and fun surprise, sometimes they just don't happen. Never mind, we had to revise the plan quickly, partly because of the worsening weather and the fact that though Jonny was keen to do a day's walking with us, his hip (from years of farm work) was not so good and they wouldn't risk a walk with us today in the wet.

The plan was get to Cadgwith Cove have lunch (in the pub with the same name as the place) and meet up there, after Jonny and Jane had driven around with their car and walked a little to join us. They'd then drive us to a drop off point on the path with the promise of visiting the Lizard pasty shop that they were keen to do. The best pasty shop in the world type claims were made. Who cared whether they were right or not, a hot pasty on a day like this sounded great to us! After that they'd take us down to the Lizard headland, depending on the rain, drop us off or take us a bit further along the coast as the walk to Mullion was some 10 miles away already and time was beginning to run against us. It was a function of meeting up with friends, just like on day one, with our timetable slipping badly due to the fun and time need for catching up which wasn't factored in so well by Chris and me.

The four of us got back to the path and had to negotiate some tricky wet walking along the undulations here are some of the most pronounced of the whole coastal path, and would be this way from now on until we hit the bay and flat beach of Hayle.

Our sense of humour hadn't left us, and with constant checking by Chris and me that the pub was open, we finally made it to the lovely stone clad, warm and dry barrooms of the Cadgwith Cove where Tess was asked as she walked (dripped) in what would we like, to which she replied "A towel please!" We had a merry lunch there (where I switched to 'Tribute' ale) and then decided to head to the Lizard pasty shop as promised, picking up some fuel for the afternoon. Jonny and Jane would run us down to the Lizard headland and we'd then walk along the biggest and most dramatic cliffs of the walk. Tess (who I found out the following day) had been walking with a metal brace to protect her knee under her waterproofs, was still keen but feeling the effects of a tough and very wet 6-7 miles. She was not the only one!

As we drove down the time factor was becoming an issue so we decided to get driven to Kynance Cove and Tess would get a lift back to the accommodation where Jonny and Jane had reserved us all a table for later as her knee was feeling the pain. My foot and left leg was suffering, but I thought it would be a simple two hours walk and I'd be okay, especially as the weather appeared to be improving and I really should do more walking - I could walk through the pain barrier! What would everyone say if they found out I'd not done every single mile as well I hear you ask? To be honest you have to be sensible and follow your instincts with this sort of issue, and it's very easy for anyone who's never walked these distances to joke and criticize, but being flexible was part of how we managed to complete the walk, as you will see especially around Land's End and Padstow for different reasons.

So it was just Chris, Jacky and I for the supposed easy last walk to the Mounts Bay B&B in Mullion, but it was not easy at all. The weather decided to get worse again and we had a difficult walk in it as well as not seeing the spectacular cliffs that our guide book said were on this part of the coast; they were hidden behind clouds of drizzle and sweeping rain and as we got further along we thought maybe we should leave the coastal footpath and follow the ordinary footpath to Mullion. The B&B would be a 2-mile hike anyway from the coast once we'd got there. Also I was really suffering and should not have done this part of the walk to give my feet a rest, but it was too late for that. I think Chris and Jacky realised my morale was sinking and could see my physical stress, hence they agreed to the shortcut. For the second time we left the coastal path we were yet again let down by inadequate signposting. Though my map reading is normally good you need landmarks to work with and at least some semblance of correct signage to tell one field/hedge/copse/wood/lane from another. But no, we were let down again and after wasting an hour's walk my feet could ill afford, we ended up back on the coastal path maybe two or three fields further along – oh how I cursed and was getting slower as we trudged along. After this we said we would not leave the coastal footpath again, unless we were forced too, which I'm afraid did happen when we were confronted by a landslide near Land's end (the council had supposedly sorted out a detour around the slide with a predictable result for us – totally lost in a farmers field!!!)

Anyway I digress as this day was my lowest and worst point of the entire walk as the food time limit was 8pm, it was getting darker and it looked we might not make it to the B&B in time. Always a potential problem and one of our reasons for choosing June/July to get the most light for early evening walking. We were wet, I was very tired, footsore, and grumpy and calling farmers who don't maintain footpaths on their land everything under the sun. Not surprisingly Jacky and Chris walked slightly ahead of me and I don't blame them, my conversation was not the best!

We finally made it to Mullion and reached the B&B at 7-30pm, with me in total silent mode with just enough time to give our wet boots and gear to the brilliant landlord who had a huge airing cupboard kitted out for exactly this, and just time to get some dry clothing on. Chris had sensibly phoned and sorted out with Tess our food order (and beer naturally) in advance, surprisingly the phone signals were pretty good here, we think because of the strategic place of the Lizard peninsula.

We had just made the food cut-off time and headed down to the bright and welcoming bar where Tess had a G&T for herself (a Moore family tradition) and had our beers ready too, a good sign for the evening. Jonny and Jane had also arrived so we could all have our planned meal. Much of the edge of my toughest day was taken off by the good humour of my walking pals and friends who help you get through almost anything if they are true and can make fun of adversity. My morale was being slowly restored by them and the beer, even if my feet weren't. However, the Facebook blog and uploading of pictures was off the chart for another day too.

Chapter 6 – Marazion

Wednesday the 3rd July 2013 dawned clearer and we were hopeful the weather would lift and after a nights rest and more running repairs to my feet and limbs I was ready to join Chris as it looked to be another eventful day. After retrieving our wonderfully dry boots and gear from the landlord, who wasn't odd or eccentric, we met Tess and Jacky for breakfast. There we roughly planned today's travel and where we would be meeting Chris's accountant – another Chris and his friend Judie, who owned a cottage down here, and who were intending on joining us for as much walking as they could whilst we were in the area. Pretty impressive as they were in their late sixties. We would be finishing and staying opposite St Michael's mount an iconic Cornish place on the south coast.

As we left Mullion the temperature seemed to rise, it started to dry out and the day looked like it would be a sunny one. Chris and I had checked the weather constantly leading up to the walk and we both knew there was a big high pressure system on its way from the Azores and if it came in we might get a whole week of decent weather – certainly after yesterday's rain my feet and morale would need it! As we passed the local links golf club we were both back in t-shirts, though the ladies remained with their waterproof gear on, probably hoping the hood's would block out Chris's detailed explanations of the golfers drives, chips and putts etc. as we walked passed the morning players out on the course. Chris being a very keen golfer, you couldn't deny his enthusiasm for the sport as he chatted and this, together with the feeling that the weather was turning in our favour added to the good vibes of the group as we trekked along.

We walked quite comfortably for this morning's session and the lovely long coast line of Porthleven beach opened up before us. We were due to meet Chris and Judie at the end, the next adventurers to join the party. We made good progress even though my right foot was not doing so well and we soon met our latest companions - well you could not miss Chris senior's bright red trousers and top as they appeared on the footpath to say hello. They were in good spirits too and were soon chatting away as we headed into Porthleven and the Harbour Inn where we intended to have a coffee (or in the case of Chris junior, a beer of course since it's an unfair temptation for a man of his calibre to go into a pub and drink coffee). Before we got there however, Chris senior had managed to walk into a hedge ditch on the way into the town, which was quite impressive after only half an hour with us and had to be hauled upright by us all after giggles galore once we realised he was ok. He was easy to find at the bottom of the siding covered in grass as the red trousers acted like a beacon to the prostrate victim! He was however, very generous and insistent that he paid for the drinks as a thank you to us and he's just one of those larger than life characters to whom this sort of thing comes naturally and his sense of humour was not dented by his fall. Judie meanwhile, had had no such problems with the walking as she'd run marathons in her youth and looked as though she could easily keep up with us, keeping a merry conversation going as we went along.

Feeling refreshed we headed out for the quite tough walk around all the dis-used mines of Rinsey Cove that dot the coastline here with dramatic views of the cliffs and coastline where they are set into the rock or on the footpath itself. Perfect backdrop for *Poldark* fans! We continued to head for Praa Sands and a late lunch as time was getting on and the walking had been slower than we thought with six people in the party, combined with my right foot issues and Tess, who was again walking with a metal knee brace to protect it as much as possible and who was also feeling the strain of the second day's continuous walk. The sun was now out and beaming down on us which was very comforting and we were all very happy to make it to Praa Sands and the Beach Comer Café that was very conveniently on the Coastal Path and beach. Our friends Jonny and Jane also joined us here for lunch so it was quite a gathering and Chris senior again insisted on paying for the drinks bill for all of us despite our protests and a final agreement that we pay for our food if he paid for the drinks – of which there were a few in the rising heat and thirst from the walk. It was a beautiful scene as the holidaymakers were on the beach and in the sea, as we were relaxing drinking cool lager and being served Japanese tempura for lunch. What a change for the Cornish cuisine from our youth of basically fish & chips and pasties (not that they aren't some of the best food ever) it's just that the choice nowadays reflects the growth and diversity of food down here. The beauty was tempered a little however, by the sight of my right foot in a plastic ice-cream tub full of ice and cold water (care of Jane) to fight the full force of my blisters and aching foot!

For the final afternoon session to Marazion we decided that Tess and I would get a taxi direct from the café to give us a rest and chance to recover, whilst Jacky and Chris would walk around Prussia Cove and the final 6 miles since it was a childhood memory of his from summer holidays down here and he felt he needed to see it again, and Jacky was very keen to keep walking. Judie also offered to sort out our laundry as we were going to use the facilities in Penzance, but she insisted and said she'd have it all back when we would all meet up the following morning in Mousehole - very kind and saving us a lot of time and hassle. She and Chris senior were heading back to her cottage to recover as well and Jonny and Jane said their goodbye's to us before returning to their own holiday, so it was an afternoon of parting of the ways.

Tess and Jacky were staying in a different location to me and Chris so we agreed after the drop off to meet up later in the Cutty Sark restaurant to celebrate their last night on the road. I checked into the Netherleigh B&B and found a pleasantly normal landlord. I then set about foot repairs and muscle rest for my legs. It was here I sat down and I realised that my preparation really had not been as good as it should have been and I was a bit worried that if things didn't improve soon it could be a big problem, especially as Chris's walking stamina was better than mine and I didn't want to hold him back. However, we had agreed at the start that if either was injured or couldn't continue the walk through illness we'd get around it, and especially if we were into a third day of walking through rain, plan B was to get the bus/taxi and sit in the pub instead. A fair alternative as we weren't doing any of this for charity, despite some people asking which one we were doing it for! It was supposed to be a holiday too, so yes, I can hear the tuts and reader disapproval of such thoughts but alternative plans and improvisation is what we were good at and getting better as we went along.

Chris and Jacky made good progress and they were in Marazion in plenty of time for the evening meal, which was one of those giggly, laugh at anything, fun nights as we reflected on our day, fellow companions and the fun we'd had. How would tomorrow go as it would be a tough terrain walk of 15 miles to Porthcurno? What a difference from the stress of the previous day and late chaos of that evening meal! I'm sure the rest and sunshine too had a made a big impact on my morale and my feet were already recovering, especially with some wine coursing through my veins and the excellent company I had too. Chris's morale had never been dented.

CHAPTER 7 – PORTHCURNO

After a good rest I was back ready for the walk with my worries of yesterday behind me, so Chris and I had breakfast and planned the new day. Always a nice thing and part of the fun of trying to come up with a plan that could easily end in tatters, especially having to meet Chris senior and Judie again and keep all six of us in one piece and walking together.

Our talk was of course in English and as we kept on chatting (speaking a little German myself) I started to notice that all the other guests were conversing in German and looking around as they came down in two's and three's around us, it felt very nice being in my old home county surrounded by a foreign language. It reminded me of our school days in Bude with foreign exchange students from as far away as Sweden (one who we'll meet later) and Norway etc. spending time with us in the long summer holidays, teaching us swear words in their language and learning important Cornish customs like how to beach party in return. It also showed us the international appeal of St Michael's Mount and the south Cornish coast. Later on in the north coastal walk, as we headed into Port Isaac and *Doc Martin* country, the German tourists would be there in numbers once more as it's quite a big hit show over there too.

As we left the B&B (no strange landlord here – perhaps the early days were not the norm then and Cornish hoteliers were in fact more normal, whatever that is?) we waited for Jacky and Tess outside and the taxi to take us through the busy City of Penzance, which we decided we didn't really need to walk through. We needed to make time up early as Jacky and Tess were heading home when we reached our destination today and couldn't really afford a long walk to Mousehole. So a taxi getting us there quickly would be best for all of us and leave Chris and I some beach time at Porthcurno. We could now see through the mist and heat haze and the signs were of another hot day ahead. The lovely island and the Mount came up through the grey mist as it all got clearer and very impressive it was too.

The local chatty taxi man soon had us through Penzance and we were dropped off in Mousehole, met up with Chris senior and Judie, started along the road and up to the footpath we went. The morning mist was drizzly and a bit damp and took longer to clear than we thought at first. We now looked back towards Newlyn and we could see Penlee point; the taxi driver had pointed out the Lifeboat disaster memorial to all those who lost their lives in the terrible storm of December 1981. It was one of those quiet moments of reflection, a realization of the power of the sea and nature and an appreciation of what an amazing job the lifeboat people do, risking their own lives and sometimes losing them to save others.

The sobering tone thinking of the disaster did not last of course, as we now had Chris senior and Judie chatting away with all of us with their happy go lucky attitude, matching Chris's continued enthusiasm and Tess and Jacky's sense of humour. We also could see the sun was trying to come out and this lifted our spirits even more. There were no falling in ditches this time as the headlands rose and fell as we trekked on towards Lamorna cove. Chris senior had a bright white jumper with black stripes today so, again, we couldn't miss him, but as with the previous day the terrain was taking its toll. My feet seemed to be back and my limbs had finally geared up to the walk so I felt fine, but we all decided that once we saw the rocks the other side of the Cove that Judie and Chris senior would walk back to their car and meet us in Porthcurno. It was a good call as we rounded each point, of which there were many, as we were rising and falling up and down the cliffs and at one point I only had a 3 foot wide path of granite rock beneath my feet, a solid rock wall to lean against and air between me and a 60-80 foot fall down to the sea-which was quite happily smashing into the rocks below – it certainly made me concentrate on exactly what I was doing. No room on these parts to make a mistake, which was quite an effort after the mileage already covered today, but we all made it through safely and comfortably in the end.

Chris senior and Judie had driven many times to Lamorna Cove and the nice café there for a pit stop coffee/tea and cake but had never walked over the cliffs from Mousehole and were amazed at the effort needed to get there by foot. A classic tourist-weekend-local driver mistake when all they do is drive to the next cove or beach around the headland car park and cafe which maybe takes 5 or 10 minutes, yet by walking could be half an hour or more of a tough climb and descent! The story of our walk so far.

For the remaining four walkers the sun was now out and beaming down making it very pleasant indeed. We were all in t-shirts or jackets with coats away or wrapped around and on we walked, coming across one of the nicest quietest little places on the coast – Penbarth Cove, complete with little stepping stones to cross the stream; we all stopped for a water break and little rest just to take in the place. From there we rounded the headland where the Logan Rock is to be seen best on the rocks jutting out at Horrace Point from Pednvounder beach. We could also see Porthcurno and its curved bay with its beach on the other side towards the Carrack Point.

We had maybe an hour's walk to go and Chris now kicked into beer mode as we'd agreed to meet at the Cable Station Inn where Tess's car was parked and he was determined to get there before Chris senior and Judie to quench his thirst! Seriously it was mainly to try and get an order in and pay for it before Chris senior had already organized our bar bill. His sudden burst of speed was impressive especially for his sister and Jacky, who were now aware of the extra mode he had available to deploy in beer situations. He smiled, waved and disappeared at a fair pace into the rather large gorse bushes and bracken that was rising all around us on this section of the path. We followed more sedately talking about the fun we'd over the last few days and both ladies said it seemed that time had almost stopped and they couldn't believe it was only a few days they'd been away.

We arrived at the pub and Chris had managed just to pip Chris senior to the bar and set up a tab so we all sat down to a pleasant late lunch, general chat and assessment of how it had all gone for our newcomers to the walk. They all agreed they'd thoroughly enjoyed it and were all envious of Chris and I who still had some eight days and 120-130 miles to go. It was quite sad to say goodbye to our fellow walkers as their cars pulled out of the car park and they headed back to their homes and lives.

Oh and in case you were wondering Judie had dropped of all our laundry, cleaned and ironed and ready for the two of us to get another four or five days towards the goal of Bude in comfort - we couldn't thank her enough and were so grateful as this was one of our biggest potential issues.

The Seaview Hotel was just up the road so we went up and checked in (normal landlord!) sorted our gear and decided that we'd have a few hours before Chris's old college pals (Steve and Martin) arrived later. There was some debate as to whether they would be walking with us or not, but that was to be resolved alongside our big problem of the next day when would have to try and walk from Porthcurno via Land's End to St Ives, a mere 25 miles around difficult terrain. We put that problem off by getting our books and walking (with no rucksack) down to the lovely beach and enjoying the sunny early evening for a few hours, whilst the holiday-makers played around on the beach. A group of American students were playing the obligatory beach Frisbee and seeming to have a great time down here in Cornwall celebrating the 4th July Cornish style and the whole place was very relaxed. At some point, as I'd lost track of time reading my book in the evening sunshine, we were greeted and disturbed from our relaxation by Chris's two old college friends who'd found us on the beach after a few texts. We went back up the hill to the Cable Station Inn for some food, drinks and lively conversation.

By the way the Cable Station Inn and the area around here has a lot of history for communication fans as the first under-sea telegraph cables (hence the name) were laid here in 1870 from Portugal, with other cables coming in at different times over the next thirty to forty years from South Africa and as far as the Azores. Though the station has long since gone, six under-sea fibre optic cables still come ashore here from as far away as the USA and it's a global link too – amazing in this little part of Cornwall. So how come our internet connections and WI-FI were so poor then?

I digress so back to our story. It turned out that Martin could drink even more than Chris and I was glad that Steve and I made no attempt to keep up. I just sat back with the old college reunion feel of the evening learning how Chris's college life at Camborne School of Art had been influenced by and with these two characters, no different from student relationships all over the world, yet all completely unique at the same time too. After many beers and games of pool we retired to the Seaview Hotel and they headed off to their accommodation after arranging that we would see the two of them again at Land's End the next day as they were staying in a different place completely and Martin was not going to be walking with us. Steve would definitely do some.

CHAPTER 8 – ST IVES

The next morning Friday the 5th July 2013 dawned as another hot sunny day and the forecast was for good weather for the whole weekend as we were up to our halfway point. I managed to write all my post cards – old school and I suppose the advent of the smart phone will mean this dies out completely as the next generation won't ever need to write anything by a pen anymore. A bit of a shame as there is something very enjoyable and tangible about getting a postcard with good pictures (in this case from local artists of scenic shots of Cornwall) and postage stamps and franking ink all over it. But the new technology does reach a larger audience so much quicker and is easy for everyone to use and to see what's going on in real time. With social media the replies and backchat add a different dimension too to holidays and trips away. Old school lecture/rant over, we went down to a very smart breakfast where we were served by a waiter who could only be described as something out of a Noel Coward play, complete with patterned waistcoat – great the eccentric host was back and normality was gone!

Our plan had to be amended for the day as we'd already agreed with Martin and Steve that they would meet us at Land's End – we had to do that iconic walk. They would then pick us up at Sennon Cove and take us to St Ives via the pub at Zennor as the now 25 odd miles in a day was not possible in this terrain and given the time constraints. Something we hadn't really worked out properly as we had squeezed a day early to finish on so we'd have the weekend to recover and return to home on the final Sunday - amazing how the plan and reality have to be constantly modified and I know you will be back tutting about the use of a car but when needs must you have to go with it. And it's a holiday not an endurance test to win a medal or for charity – otherwise we would of course have been cheating!

Chris and I soon re-joined the coastal path right at the famous open air Minack Amphitheatre, which loomed up to our left on the cliffs and looked very impressive as we headed towards Porthgwarra beach in the morning sunshine. The Channel and the Atlantic Ocean were now in front of us and it was the first time it had been just the two of walking together for a few days. We were in good spirits and the legs, feet and backs carrying the rucksacks were all in working order and it felt good to be heading to Land's End – roughly the half-way mark and the turning point towards the North Coast.

There was one incident on the way to Lands' End we need to share and that was the talking hedge man. Yes we found a talking hedge! There had been a small landslide on the coastal path on the way around Porthgwarra and the local council had diverted us through a village and farmers' fields around the obstacle. As usual it was badly sign-posted and we got lost (there was a family going the opposite direction asking us which way they should go and we weren't much help to them as they were lost too). Grumbling and mumbling we ended up in a field corner with two huge hedges and no idea of where to go. To our left the hedge suddenly had a voice with someone saying loudly "It's this way to the coastal path!" What a talking hedge we both thought? As we leaned over the top there was a man there with his walking gear, rucksack, sat-nav and a tan that made his skin look like leather striding along the deep overgrown gully on the other side. No hello are you lost, can I help? He just repeated "It's this way, follow me". So we did, clambering through the hedge and fighting our way through the overgrown farm lane until we did indeed arrive back at the path. Thank you talking hedge man as he strode off at a tremendous pace and that was the last we saw of him.

We took some good photos of the coast as we went along passed Gwenapp Head and talked about the plan for the rest of the day as we had to get to the Atlantic Hotel in St Ives and were still wondering what best to do, but Steve and Martin already had the whole day well organized as we found out shortly. Upon rounding Mill Bay and seeing the iconic cluster of the Land's End buildings ahead we started to increase the pace a bit and Chris was using his long site to try and see what was ahead and whether the coastal path carried on around or would we be forced inland etc. Neither of us could remember from our previous visits by road, what bits were free and accessible and what bits were privatized and not.

In the distance he spotted what looked like a no entry sign meaning we'd have to detour around the buildings to the road and away from the path. A lot of grumbling and moaning from both of us about this being of a point of national interest and that Land's End should be open and free to all and the development should be controlled, environmentally adapted and smartened up etc. How grumpy do we sound? All part of the ageing process when you get to fifty, I here you all say… However, as we got closer there seemed to be a tent and table set up with two people waving at us and the sign now looked like a road sign with a number 50 on it – what on earth was this? Then we recognized it was Martin and Steve and they'd set up a little drinks table with food and some champagne. They'd made a sign exactly like the tourist Land's End one, you know with your town or city on it and how many miles away you are from it. The number 50 road sign (denoting our age) was headed by a marker with "They're round the bend" and the date underneath and another sign post on it with the left hand side "Has been here" pointing to where we walked from and a right hand side "Moore to go" pointing towards the coastal path we hadn't walked yet. Really funny and a nice touch from his old pals. Martin was here with work as well as pleasure as he has something to do with the Company down here that ran the catering and leisure bit and had blagged kit and permission to set it all up for us, so we proceeded to have a drink of champagne to celebrate and discuss what we would do next.

The plan was simple, Chris and I would finish the day's walk at Sennen Cove 3-4 miles away so a shortish walk, where the guys would meet us at the Mayon Old Coastguard Lookout point and we would then spend some time on the beach. Martin had some more work to do and Steve needed to get his car and accommodation sorted as he hadn't managed to get booked into the hotel we were staying at in St Ives, and the hotels and B&B's were filling up due to the good weather. So off we went towards Sennen cove and as I said, the place was packed when we finally got there for a nice little two hour swim and relax on the beach. It was our only swim of the trip and we both had an idea in our heads that we could have done this each day, but the reality of the walk and time meant it wasn't something we could afford to do, sadly. I think we had the idea of reliving our formative years where we spent most summers like this down the beach, a very lucky and not fully understood or appreciated at the time way of growing up indeed.

With the weather being so good and the forecast was for a great weekend the whole world had started to head to any beach and the coast wherever that was – including Sennen. Steve stayed with us while Martin went off to do some more work back at Lands' End. Eventually Martin returned with his car after an hour or so and we then all drove off to the village of Zennor and the famous pub The Tinners Arms for a late lunch. These three guys had spent quite a lot of their college lives nipping down from Camborne to this great pub and the village is very picturesque too. So after a few beers and much reminiscing from the college days and enjoying the country pub outdoors in the sun it was time to head to St Ives and the Atlantic Hotel.

Here we would be meeting Chris's golfing crew who had agreed to come down by train on the Friday, join us for Saturday and Sunday walking, then returning back to their lives and jobs in the south east on the Monday. Chris's brother in law Huw would also be joining us for the weekend too, since after missing out on the Coverack trip with Tess he was very keen to get walking.

So after introductions galore we all checked in (big proper hotel, no weird/odd landlord's here which was now becoming slightly disappointing) we got ourselves sorted and all met up downstairs for food and it was a merry throng for the evening meal, followed by a trip to the local pub The Cornish Arms.

Steve had not been able to get a room here though, so had got a room across town and would join us for the following day's hike to Portreath, an old stomping ground for the three Camborne School of Art alumni.

After the evening events Martin was leaving us to head home (a busy man) so we wished him well with lots of thanks for the fun around Land's End and a safe journey back up country and we all retired for the night.

Chapter 9 – Portreath

The next day was another sunny one for Saturday the 6th of July 2013 and I still had done very little (none in fact) blogging on the Facebook page but I resolved (if the WI-FI connection was up to it) I would start tonight as the congratulation texts for reaching Lands' End - *Where on earth are you? Which pub is it you've visited now? Are you still alive?* - were prompting us to be a bit more communicative with our audience!

The walking party organized itself well this morning considering the numbers and we all headed off in a good mood past Carbis Bay railway station, down the hill to join the coastal path and head around the bay and along to the flat river estuary and town of Hayle. We now numbered a magnificent seven with Huw, Mike, Conor, Geoff, Steve, Chris and myself all gearing up for the day's walk ahead. Walking poles were in evidence, convinced they are efficient, big leather walking boots, all sorts of socks, rucksacks, packs, water bottles, food and all the evidence of organized chaos as we trekked along the footpath.

The bay to our left was an absolutely magnificent stretch of flat golden sand as far as the eye could see and we quickly made it over the river and around the town of Hayle. It was quite a tough walk through the dunes the other side and if any of you want to up your fitness training and are able, head to a sandy beach and dunes and use this as it really tests your stamina.

We were on a mission now to reach one of the most iconic places in Cornwall - Godrevy point, a beautifully photogenic island with an old lighthouse. But we were also getting to know each other, how did you all meet up, what are your family circumstances, do you like football, what's your walking ability like etc. So it was good fun for that alone and the good weather and atmosphere was one of lots of blokes on an away day jolly talking rubbish.

Walking along the Gwithian Towens beach we spotted a café for lunch that had the Scottish and Cornish flags waving at the entrance, as it turned out the owner was a Scot who moved down here, a bit of a theme of waifs and strays getting to Cornwall and never quite leaving methinks. The gang were also interested in catching up on the last remnants of the British Lions rugby game with Australia where the interested parties managed to get the last fifteen minutes of a great victory and were very happy as we all sat around the café drinking a cold beer and eating an excellent lunch. It was one of those really hard places to get up from and get moving when we were all settled, but there was a fair walk ahead around the Godrevy Point headland and the lovely coastal heritage stretch and into Portreath. So after lots of prompting and rounding up the (now) veteran walkers (me and Chris) got the guys moving before their legs seized up.

Once we got going there were some excellent opportunities for photos both of us, and the lighthouse on the little island off the coast. The walk was really good as we went up and down some fantastic terrain and the sea was so calm to our left that we were all enjoying the whole day immensely. As we got towards the last headland and before we started the descent into the town we spotted a guy with a dog heading up the hill towards us. He looked very familiar to Chris and I and it soon turned out that our school friend Tim Martindale and his golden retriever Finlay were on the footpath! He'd been given our detailed plan previously with an open invitation to join us and was also a keen walker and got the dates from our Facebook page. He'd done a bit of calculation and worked out where we'd be and here we were. He is a graphic artist and having been down at St Michael's Mount the previous day had a bit of work to do up around Godrevy so was taking advantage of the good weather too. When he does this he travels in his big camper van with Finlay and then can use this as his accommodation and mobility to get those early morning/late evening/night-time shots us mere mortal's dream of.

Anyway it was a really nice surprise and we were all happy for him and Finlay to join us now and for our evening meal and beers in Portreath, at the Bassett Arms. We nipped in there for a refreshing beer as it was at the bottom of the footpath and seemed to invite us in as we headed down towards the town. We had a simple plan - get to our accommodation (Chris, Huw and I were in a separate guest house from the golfing gang) check in, shower etc. and then back to the Bassett Arms for the evening. Chris's work partners Andy and Grum (men and their nick names eh!) had now also joined us to make the weekend crew the biggest gang of the whole walk! Grum is a bit of techie wizard and had already followed us via sat nav, through Chris's iPhone (?) and was placing our whereabouts on the Facebook page at various points, so he was very helpful for our social media audience…someone knew where we were at last!

We were staying at the Dolphin Guest House and found it very easily with Chris's local knowledge and it was one of the best accommodations of the whole walk. Really modern, bright, clean, best shower of the trip and organized to the point where we even had fresh homemade cakes in our room too. The landlady was a very gregarious character who chatted with a slight Cornish accent and made us feel very welcome - no sign of an odd-ball which again was sort of disappointing, However, it was easily made up for by the enthusiasm she expressed for our walk and what we'd done so far and what we were going to do next.

The evening at the pub was a bit of a riot in terms of strangers and old friends chatting, drinking, laughing and enjoying the night as well as making the landlord a huge wodge of extra takings in the process! There was even music, dancing and at one point nearly the obligatory fight!

Cornwall attracts its fair share of waifs and strays from anywhere in the world as we know. People who fall in love with it on holiday, or work a summer and find they want to stay, other people who end up there because it's a long way away from their home and troubles and problems, all sorts of life reasons and we were used to it growing up with these characters that do make it a slightly off-beat place.

Anyway this guy, a pub local but with a strong South East/London accent so a naturalized outsider whom the landlord seem to know, came out to where we were sitting. He was obviously pretty tanked up and determined to prove he could annoy and swear at the gang of newcomers to his pub and was being obnoxious to the point where Chris and I, as hosts, needed to act. So with years of near scrapes and experience of bar room incidents behind us we took him on with the double move of Chris in front talking him down and me moving around his back and to the side in case it kicked off, checking there wasn't a gang of locals looking for fight too. As I got up and moved around this guy I could see the landlord was very anxiously watching the event, but we used our height (Chris and I are both 6ft 2") and physical presence to tell (intimidate) this guy to basically stop being an idiot and go back inside, which he did grumbling and mumbling to himself and stumbling around with his pint in hand. We all breathed a collective sigh of relief and returned to the fun. Why do you get these characters and what are they on?

We continued to enjoy the rest of the evening and were out very late revelling in the atmosphere and weather and making sure the Landlord knew we'd kept the peace and before long it was time to turn in and get ready for the shorter walk to St Agnes on the Sunday.

Chapter 10– St Agnes

The 7th of July 2013 dawned bright and clear and very warm and it would be an historic day for the tennis fans amongst us and for the walkers a tough but enjoyable part of the coast, for all of us except Conor.

Once the mighty gang had finished breakfast, paid their bills, got assembled and sorted out the plan, we would all head to the Blue Bar at Porthtowan beach for lunch, and then onto St Agnes head and down into St Agnes itself. We'd go at our own pace and not try and keep in one big group and started out up the hill and onto the coastal path. As we got to the top someone spotted a grey seal down on the beach below and we all (apart from Conor) rushed over to the cliff edge (what a bunch of tourists) and watched the seal sunning itself on the isolated shore below.

We'd noticed Conor had sat down on the clifftop bench and seemed off colour and we thought initially that the Saturday night had caught up with him but after Chris sat down with him and chatted it turned out he was suffering from vertigo, had done all his life and didn't realize how big the Cornish cliffs were - seeing us all on the edge had made him ill and stressed. So now we had a tough call to make as he couldn't face the coastal walk. We decided that Chris would walk the road route with him to Porthtowan and the rest of us would do the coastal path by the old tin mines around the headlands. We all felt sorry for him since he'd been brave enough to give the walk a go and I think the flat beach of Hayle had lulled him into thinking he'd be fine for the cliffs, but it's hard for us to appreciate the size and scale of the topography of the coast compared to elsewhere as it's such a part of Chris and my lifetime's DNA.

As we continued on up and down the steep hills we noticed to the right RAF Portreath and the MOD's weird radar buildings (circular green blobs!) all over the fenced off hillside and down into the airport itself – all off limits, but not stopping the path. The views were great out to sea the other way and the guys all seem to really relax and just enjoy the pure strange human-made buildings and quietness of the disused mines, against the natural spectacle on the other side. There were lots of comments about time standing still and how you forget where you are and just enjoy the moment, the best reason of going on any walk, wherever that turns out to be. Note *Poldark* fans you need to do this part of the walk.

After what seemed a long and tough ascent we made it over another peak and saw the village of Porthtowan below with Chris and Conor already there enjoying a pint, so down we walked and joined in the pit stop lunch/brunch. Today was the shortest walk of the whole journey but that was part of the plan as the weekenders needed a big place to stop for accommodation, whilst we had more friends coming down on the Sunday - my footballing friend Mike and his family, and our school acquaintance Adrian and his family would all be meeting us later too, so St Agnes fitted the bill for all sorts of reasons. Our fitness and stamina had increased but we were aware that others (Huw and his very tough leather walking boots especially) were suffering a bit as I'd done earlier in the walk, after a day of serious walking and on day two not giving your feet their normal chance to rest, so a 7 mile trek seemed to be the right thing to do.

We all returned to the path and walked up and around Chapel Porth beach and its café (serving excellent ice-creams) and then up and onto St Agnes Head and a view of the excellent beach crammed with tourists and then the descent into the town. The gang had had a good walk and even Conor had recovered so we all got settled in to our various overnight accommodation places and agreed to meet up later for our evening meal. We had a fair walk up the main road from the beach to the St Agnes hotel but it was where we were meeting our other friends and had made good time and soon settled in to a very big room with decent facilities. Chris had to leave and meet Adrian as he'd arranged and I had about two hours before I'd be meeting Mike, Sue and Katherine in the downstairs bar later.

It was the day of Andy Murray's famous Wimbledon final and we were aware of the implications of the event should he win and though I was tempted to nip back to the beach for an hour's swim, as a general sports fan I felt it my duty to watch his last few games and see if he'd win his first historic Wimbledon championship and not blow it, like previously. After that I'd meet up with my old friend Mike Gibb whom I'd known for over ten years from our five-a-side football up in Harpenden. He would be walking with us as far as Harlyn Bay whilst his wife Sue, and their daughter Katherine would be doing their own touristy things. Sue's comments to Mike were "Oh no not Cornwall, it always rains there", but she could not deny the weather was superb and forecast to be so for their time here. As absolute mad tennis fans they all got to watch Andy Murray's win too, which put her in a very happy mood, as the journey down by car was fine and they arrived in plenty of time to watch the tennis.

We all met up back down at the Driftwood Spars later and once more the evening was a merry one with Mike joining us and everyone in a de-mob happy mood for a good two days walking. The pub chat was about how they would all like to give up their day jobs and copy Tim or do something like it, driving around Cornwall in a van with a dog, taking pictures for a living. They were also very tempted to ring their work and try and wangle another day or two with us as they'd got the walking bug now and the weather looked fine for the next week. I think it was the beer talking of course, but there was a genuine feeling of envy that Chris and I still had five more days ahead of us and whether they could get away with it somehow they would love to join us. This was very unlikely however, trains were already booked, family's awaiting returns and work needs were pressing, so the Monday morning train back to London was probably not going to be missed.

One thing they did miss was the glorious red sunset that you get at the sea on hot sunny days like today. I took my friend Mike down to the beach at around 10pm so he could watch as the great white ball of the sun and sky go orange, then red and then see it sinking below the horizon as the fireball shimmered at sea level. Something you just can't do away from the sea. He even took a great shot of me with the red light in the background shining through on St Agnes beach. When we returned to the throng in the pub, who'd all stayed in drinking, they said we'd photo-shopped the pictures and it couldn't have been that red and orange. Well if you ever are in Cornwall on the north coast, just face west at the end of a clear hot summer's day between 9-30pm and 11pm and you'll see what I mean.

Later that night Chris, Mike, Huw and I bade farewell to the golfing gang. They were all heading off in the early morning to get their cabs and train from St Austell back to London. The four of us then walked back to the St Agnes Hotel up the long hill and in for a night cap in the hotel bar, that went on far too long. It was encouraged by the owner (another non-native from the South East familiar theme type) who was very keen on making us drink a few shots he'd made up and talk rubbish with him and the locals who were still up. Good we were back to eccentric landlords once more, though Mike was a bit concerned about his walking ability being affected by all this in the morning, which was a fair point, and you'll see whether he was right or not in the next chapter.

Chapter 11 – Crantock

Monday the 8th July 2013 dawned fine and clear once more. We sorted breakfast and our bills, being wished good luck by the staff and we geared up with rucksacks arranged and sun cream slapped on for the days hike to the lovely village of Crantock. None of us showed any effects of the night before and Chris and I assured Mike that the walking burned up all calories consumed very easily whichever way they had been introduced into your system. Huw however, had had enough walking and left us to walk on as a three, the boots and distance had taken its toll and his feet needed a good rest. He was going to be picked up at the hotel by Tess, as arranged, later.

Off we went down the road towards the coastal path and to the right of the town. It took us passed the Blue Hills Tin area and down to Trevellas Cove where we made sure we were all good and getting the pace of walking together, as being a three instead of the weekend gang, it seemed all quiet and peaceful. Mike then stormed ahead as we got to the top of the first cliff ascent, I think very keen to see the sea and was powering towards the edge and oblivion. Great, how was I going to explain to Sue that we'd lost Mike over the cliff edge within an hour of starting out from St Agnes? So a quick shout of keep to the path and check the edge very carefully before you get near it was required. Anywhere near the cliff edges you should lie down and crawl slowly towards it, so you don't walk onto the grass overhang that may seem solid but cannot support your weight, and over you go onto the rocks below! Mike fortunately did not go over the edge and heeded our warning.

After the edge encounter we made good progress as Mike is fairly fit and runs regularly as well as playing football with me once a week, and we all enjoyed the company and chat and made it safely to the World War Two ruins of Gligga Head and Wolframite Mine. This was interesting blocks of concrete ruins with fantastic views across the sea and the coast towards Newquay and it had the metal rusting gun emplacement runners all still in place too, excellent for history nerds like me and Mike. Apparently tungsten was mined here pre and during the war and had been a mining spot for a very long time in the past too. Looking out we could see the long stretch of Perran sands that we would be walking along in the afternoon, but that would come after our planned lunch in Perranporth, where we would meet up with Tess once more and Chris's mum who'd both made the trip down from Bude to meet us, picking up Huw from St Agnes on the way.

It was great to see Tess again (no walking leg brace or rucksack in sight) and Chris's mum who I hadn't seen probably since our school days. She remembered me and the parties I attended back then and we all had a very pleasant lunch at the Perranporth Inn. Sadly it was the last time I saw Chris's mum as she is no longer with us, but her words to us as we left were "Well done for the walk so far and make sure you look after each other". Tess had brought medical supplies, bags of encouragement and huge amounts of jealousy that we were still walking and she wasn't. However, she talked about her and Jacky's days with us as one of the most enjoyable things she'd done and she would have loved to re-join the march to Bude if she could.

After our goodbyes from the happy lunch and Chris's family disappearing back to the beach, we crossed the river and headed up into the sand dunes and then onto the 5 mile stretch of beach that would take us to Holywell bay and the superb coastline before we descended into Crantock beach itself and the road up to the pretty village. It was a good walk and the pace was pretty good and as we reached the end of the long flat beach of Perran sands we saw what only can be described as a dancing druid type character on the dunes edge, leaping around and shouting with who knows what substances pumping around his body, you see it all down here. A lifetime of experience teaches you just to ignore them, as long as they appear harmless, which he did, and on we went.

Mike was keen to look out for quiet beaches as we went onto the cliffs once more for Sue and Katherine so he could visit with them later on in their holiday after he'd finished walking with us and we found an excellent one at Polly Joke beach, a lovely inlet away from the main tourist trails. This was after we'd passed the old Royal Marine Training camps and the Wheal Golden disused mine and some of the best coast you can see anywhere. He was also getting distracted by all the surf schools and surf academies and the obvious surf mania that was beginning to build around us as we were heading to the opposite river side of UK's surfing top spot, Newquay. Originating from Liverpool and living and working inland in the south east for most of his life, he soon started along with comments of "I might have a go at that, it looks fun, it can't be that difficult can it?" as he gazed mesmerized at the boards and surfers out and about in Holywell and Crantock bay. Not appreciating the years of practise you need to really be good at it and how difficult it was, but I was very encouraging with comments of "Go on then Mike, do it, it will be fun".

We passed a really good ice-cream van that had already come up with an "Andy Murray's Winner" flavour combo to cash in on the previous days victory – it doesn't take the hawkers long to jump on a band wagon opportunity, but they took our mickey taking remarks well and produced a quality ice-cream for us to chomp on the way into Crantock bay. We had enough time for a sit down and paddle here as the "Garden Cottage" where we were staying was about a mile's walk uphill and away from the path into the well-kept and pretty Crantock village, and we thought our feet deserved a cool dip in the ocean after a hard days walking and a half an hour sit down.

We got up slowly and walked up the beach road passed the thatched roofs and stone houses and cottages, complete with two village pubs in the middle. Very chocolate box England with Cornish stone. The owners of the Garden Cottage, once we'd located it, were very welcoming as we were the only three guests staying that night, well it was a Monday and not school holidays. They had a pot of tea ready for us and were quite happy to chat about what we were up to and explain what was available in the village. Both from London, they had ended up down here running the B&B, the familiar theme for our landlords continued.

After sorting out our gear and rooms we headed into the village and ate a pleasant meal at the Cornishman pub and we even spotted a café that did vegetarian and vegan food, which was very handy for Mike as his wife and daughter were vegetarians, so the village got a bonus from him to relay back to them in Newquay and also another example of the change down here with regards to food from our youth. More up to date catering for varied tastes instead of just giving the vegetarians a cheese salad and hoping that was enough, oh the bad old days!

Another relaxing evening was spent with just the three of us chatting and drinking in the evening sunshine and it was quite a contrast to the last few nights of big parties. I think Chris appreciated it as he'd had a lot more hosting to do than I had and I did feel a bit guilty on one level, but we'd both managed to get through the trials and tribulations of the walk and people logistics so far, with no disasters, and he seemed to be enjoying the quietness and calmness of this night. We'd even chatted to an English family at the pub who lived in Geneva and were down on holiday with their new-born, and talked about country pubs, the seaside, and English beer which were some of the things they really missed living in Switzerland. I mention them as they will re-appear in our next chapter, more of that later. Finally we got to do some blogging on the Facebook page, amazing I hear you say, and you can only have so much of a good thing, we also uploaded enough pictures to satisfy the three or so people who were following us, I think.

CHAPTER 12 – HARLYN BAY

Tuesday the 9th July 2013 was an even hotter day than before. We'd got up nice and early in order to cross the river Gannel via the Penpol footbridge as it was a big tidal river and if we didn't get the timing right we'd be walking a 4 mile detour. After an excellent breakfast we headed off in good spirits down to the bay. The heat haze was noticeable being on such a big river estuary, but we knew the sun would soon burn it all off as the day got hotter. Nipping across the bridge and into the other side we clambered up a very steep hill and into the first real urban area since Penzance. We'd decided to not go around the Fistral and west side but go through the town as quickly as we could avoiding the golf course and heading East through the shops and streets of Newquay to the coastal path just passed the Porth Beach Holiday Park. The town was buzzing but also seemed to be very relaxed in the heat and we made easy progress through it, though it seemed odd walking back into towns with high street shops, and all the normal urban roads, pavements etc. We were quite glad to be back out onto the headlands once more and the long stretch of coast over Watergate bay. It looked stunning in front of us and we'd decided that Mawgan Porth would be the lunch time stop which was at the end of the 3 mile beach.

After the trek around Beacon cove and the Beryl's point we descended into Mawgan Porth having to adapt to an ever increasing heat and sunshine we stumbled across the aptly named "Merrymoor Inn" on the roadside and decided we'd lunch here. Mike and Chris got a table in the garden area and I ordered the drinks and food, with the bar staff looking very exhausted and tired from a weekend that I think was non-stop from Friday to Monday. By the looks of the crowds at the beach it would be another long hot day for them. So back in the garden we chatted about the next bit of the walk and the pub was filling up fast. In walked the family from Geneva from the previous night and they had their new-born and were struggling to find a table as there were no shady tables left, so we waved them over to us and gave them our table with the shady umbrella. They were very grateful and offered us a free drink as recompense. Mike and Chris flatly refused on principle of their needs with the baby were more than ours. Whereas I was more of the one good turn deserves another and was about to say thanks, are you sure, ok, great I'll order another drink, when I realised it would not be good to argue with my two pals and kept quiet. So this could have been a world's first of Chris actually refusing the offer of a drink (for all the right reasons of course!). After their gratitude and an excellent lunch we got packed, waved the family from Geneva goodbye and started across the river and up the other side to walk along the Bedruthen Steps.

It was a great walk and the scenery was fantastic, it's a National Trust (NT) part of the coast too so there are some good facilities along here for all our needs, except for Mike's ice-cream. For the third or fourth time since St Agnes he was not happy with the ice-cream he'd been given at the shop and our pit stop break. He was going on about Cornish ice-cream being supposedly so good, which it is, so why don't they taste like it then? I found out the problem, Mike was being hood-winked by the advertising of weird and wonderful flavours that sounded great (raspberry and passionfruit with a hint of mulberry and hazelnut blah-blah, you know what I mean) instead of going for the basic vanilla or rum and raisin type, which is much simpler and tastes better, personal view of course.

Returning to the walk we continued on admiring the superb views and it seemed at one point we were the only three people on the coast as everyone had not ventured very far from the NT car park area on the top. We now had to make a tough decision that was one of those, it looks possible on the map, 6 miles extra round via Trevose Head and back, but could we do it as time was against us? Mike had to meet his family in Harlyn Bay at a reasonable time later and Chris and I had to think about the laundry situation once more and did we really have two to three hours spare to cover the ground? We could make it via a big push but Mike and Chris thought not, I agreed and then had one of those yes but moments. Throughout all my youth and growing up I'd seen the Trevose Head Light House beaming across the sea from Bude and my home village of Poughill and had never been there and was saying my fourteen year old self would never forgive me as I was so close to it now. Come on we ought to make a go for it and made my appeal to my fellow walkers, with which they concurred, ok let's go for it.

We soon realised we'd have to up the pace drastically which Chris and Mike seemed to do with ease and I suddenly realised that I didn't have an extra gear or the stamina in the heat to keep up with them. It's amazing how each body is so different and that even though my walking fitness was very high, the heat and my build and stamina were not right for the extra pace, whereas Chris and Mike were. So we agreed to abandon the trek after thirty minutes of hard walking and head for Harlyn bay as planned without going around the Trevose headland. A deep regret inside but I promised myself I will return here one-day in the future and walk the ground. I also had to put up with some mickey taking comments from my two fellow walkers and quite right too and that's all part of the fun.

We made it to Tryarnon Bay and now had to cross north eastwards via the Constantine bay roads and holiday/caravan park camps-ville, that seem to sprawl around here as far as the eye could see. After checking with the cafes and a tea pit stop no-one seemed to know how we'd get through the maze. Everyone we spoke to was a tourist who'd come by car and many had no idea what the Coastal path was or where Harlyn Bay was either. Following our directional sense, using the map and a bit of luck we got through to Harlyn Bay, which was very calm and quiet and we made our way through the coastal path once more to the Harlyn Inn. Here we met up with Sue and Katherine to relay our stories of the last two days and have a pleasant farewell drink with Mike before they all headed back to Newquay and the rest of their holiday later.

So it was back to just Chris and I once more and our pressing laundry problem was about to be solved. We were at that point where the laundry would be able to walk its own way to Bude as it was probably alive by now and we always knew we'd need to get everything washed at least twice for the trip and politely asked the young manager in charge if he could help and we'd pay for the laundry work that needed doing. He was great and as a regular cyclist he knew exactly what we needed on our trip, "Here's a black bin liner, put it all in there and I'll get it back to you later or early in the morning, no charge, oh and it won't be ironed either." We were very grateful and knew this would be enough to get us home now and settled down to our evening meal and a relaxing beer.

The place was very much pile 'em high, sell it low type place and our room was absolutely boiling from the days sun. The shower didn't work very well either but we were not going to complain after the laundry offer, the place was clean, and the beds comfortable so we settled down for texting, blogging and generally sorting out our gear. It would be fun tomorrow as we had to walk through and across Padstow to Rock and then onto Port Isaac (*Doc Martin* world) via the toughest part of the whole walk, a 9 mile undulating cliff walk with literally nothing other than the natural beauty between the two towns. Still the two walkers were geared up for it.

Chris then received a call from our old school friend Chris Mill asking if he could join us for the walk tomorrow. He's a farmer and holiday cottage owner and had been working fourteen hour days in the heat for the last week to get the silage harvested and fancied a break with us, to walk, talk, drink beer and have a day out of the tractor cab if possible? So we said yes straight away of course, and then had to think about the logistics of meeting up and decided we'd meet him in Rock where his wife Tracey could drop him off and we'd all meet up at Port Gaverne after the walk. The thinking caps were on as we knew we couldn't walk to Rock in enough time to get the whole day's trek done in a day, wait for Chris to get down from north of Bude and end up at our booked accommodation of the Cornish Arms which was already a 2-3 mile walk away from Port Isaac. We thought this would be a very tough day anyway. What were we to do? Well it was time to use public transport and agree that Tracey would drop us off at the end, otherwise we couldn't fit it all in sensibly. I can hear the tuts and moaning about the not walking everywhere bit, and yes we would miss the headland of Stepper Point and Hawker's Cove, but friendship was calling and the Port Isaac day would be as adventurous as all the others as you'll see.

CHAPTER 13 – PORT ISAAC

Wednesday 10th July was another scorcher and even though we were up early the heat haze was already being burnt away. Our laundry had been retrieved the night before, all washed, dried and packed so we could get an early breakfast and head via the local bus to Padstow, catch the ferry across the huge river Camel estuary to meet our new guest walker. We were the only people down for breakfast despite the place being full and we thanked the manager for his help as we left. He was organising surfers outside for the day ahead and wished us luck for the rest of the walk and he didn't have a generic south east accent either, so not in the mould of other landlords.

The local bus service was on time and excellent, not cheap but we needed to get to Rock by 10am or so to meet up with our friend and give us a chance to get the walk done to Port Isaac done in a sensible time. There were lots of pensioners using the route and we seemed the only people under seventy on the bus, but we didn't mind as it whizzed along the B3276 and it dropped us off right in the heart of Padstow. Finding our way to the outer harbour and the ferry across to Rock was easy and we had a nice 15-20 minute sun bathe whilst we waited for the returning ferry and boarding with the other tourists. Padstow is a lovely place to visit and we were a bit sad we weren't going to experience it, but we have both been here a few times before and therefore didn't feel too bad about just passing through.

In no time at all we were dis-embarking on the Rock side of the estuary and there was Chris and Tracey literally just parking up and saying our hellos. We were offered Saffron cakes and to take our rucksacks for the day, which I took up and Chris didn't. He just felt he'd done so much with it and it helped his walking rhythm he would rather keep it. I just took the opportunity to save some energy, which turned out that I would need in bucket loads on this day as it progressed, and also partook of the Saffron cakes, too. A big reminder of Cornwall and the bright radio-active yellow cakes that tasted really good. So all sorted we set off at a good pace. There is a picture of Chris Mill and me looking almost identical, similar white tea shirts, dark shades, pale green shorts, height and build with almost matching walking boots, marching along the sand edge of the beach walk to Polzeath around the headland. The weirdest thing of all was that for three hours it felt as though I still had the rucksack on my back, even though it wasn't physically there, my muscle memory and twelve days of walking had imprinted it in my mind and body and couldn't shake it off for hours.

With the temperature rising we definitely needed to make sure our water was full and we knew that once we'd gone around Pentire point passed Polzeath there was only a NT water tap at Port Quin between us and Port Isaac. The sea was dead calm as was the non-existent breeze and we made decent progress and were happily chatting away telling Chris Mill of our adventures and catching up on his life and what had been happening to various characters of our past, as you do. After a couple of hours we made it to the said Tap and had just missed the mobile café van that appears here from time to time to provide refreshments and food, damn, though water was our main concern as we'd get something to eat when we made it to Port Isaac. Though in hindsight, a wonderful thing, I should have maybe stacked up some more saffron cakes as I ran out of puff as we headed towards Port Isaac itself. Once we'd drunk our fill and refilled the water bottles from the tap we headed off to some of the remotest bits of the coastal walk and some serious undulations in the topography.

However, the air was not moving at all and as we got further along towards civilisation and the farmed field boundaries the grass and crops were chest high and not allowing any air at all to circulate. To me it felt absolutely stifling and the heat continued to rise. I was really struggling for air at one point and had to sit down with both Chris's concerns at my shape as I was in a bit of a bad way for probably ten or fifteen minutes or so until I'd got my breath back properly. Nearly six hours in the heat was taking its toll. The conditions were fierce and I don't know if you remember but the SAS tragedy of the 13th July 2013 in the Brecon Beacons was only three days ahead of this day and suffering as I was with these conditions, I can see clearly how the accident would have happened in this weather as nothing changed in this respect for the next three days in the south of the UK too. Hot, dry, very calm, flat seas and no air breezes to speak of.

Recovering my breath and spirits we finally made it into Port Isaac passing the iconic Doc Martin's cottage (that is a private residence in real life). I had to stand in front of and get a picture for my wife who was a fan of the programme. Talking of fans of the programme wet met a German tourist couple with their dog in tow heading up to the coastal path and they asked us about what the walk was like, how far could they go along? We said that the views were excellent, but that it would be very tough for the dog and it was a very long way to the water. Our advice was not to try and do it in the heat with the dog, go for short walk to get the great views and they seem to take it on board. Or maybe they saw my physical shape and thought *these guys have a point*.

As we headed down the steep hill into the beautiful Cornish village of Port Isaac, home of the *Fisherman's Friends* folk singers, picture post-card beauty surrounding us, Chris was into beer refreshment mode whilst Chris Mill and I were in any food please mode and charged up from the bottom of the harbour to the superbly placed pasty shop. "I'm sorry they're not hot" said the shop lady, that didn't matter to us as we paid for the lovely big pasties and proceeded to chomp them at breakneck speed. We then had to follow beer mode Chris who was striding ahead up the hill to the Old School Hotel (yes *Doc Martin* fans, the TV school in the village is a Hotel now in the real world) and its friendly looking outside bar area. It was also the first watering hole that was open on our way through the town and Chris had already spotted this fact, he had not indulged in our pasty pursuits, he can live off air and beer alone.

Arriving at the bar it seemed completely empty to us as we looked at the row of beer taps and bottles with not a bar staff person in sight. What we didn't realise in our rush to quench our thirst was the landlady sitting behind us in a corner feeding her baby. She was silent and didn't say a word and was sitting patiently observing us though we didn't know it.

I thought Chris was going to start harrumphing as we were keen for a drink but fortunately a young women soon came out to serve us, looking very nervous and apologising for being elsewhere. She was not a local and turned out she was a student and this was her summer job working down here. It was also the first pint she was about to try and pull ever! Which of course made her very nervous and self-conscious with three beer veterans in front of her. So we offered to help and teach her to angle the glass, pour slowly, etc. and encouraging her so she didn't make a hash of her first drawn pint. And then proceeded to get her to pour the next two pints on her own, slowly and carefully and getting her to chat away as you do to remove the nerves and get our beers quickly and she did a fine job. After which the landlady suddenly piped up behind us making us jump saying she'd seen the whole thing and complementing us on our helpful attitude, incredible beer knowledge and encouragement to the young staff member, who was thankful too.

Feeling very virtuous and incredibly thirsty we sat outside drinking a wonderful cold lager overlooking the bay in three seconds flat, well maybe twenty…After a good sit down rest we deserved, we then headed off to meet Chris Mill's wife Tracey at the Port Gaverne Hotel on the other side of town. Mainly because the traffic issues in Port Isaac are horrendous, especially if you don't know your way around a fishing village where some roads are less than a car's width, yes there are places in the world pre-car, and some roads are at 45 degree slopes into and out of the harbour.

We were soon with Tracey again and I was re-united with my rucksack once more. In good spirits and after another beer and chat we'd arranged for Chris and Tracey to come back later for their evening meal with us and they'd get their son to drive them back down as a bonus too, responsible drivers and cashing in on their taxi runs they'd done for the kids in the past. Getting dropped off at a suitable place, as they headed back towards Bude, we then walked the short distance to the Cornish Arms at Pendoggett and got settled into our accommodation, which was good. Both of us caught up with our families and our social media responsibilities and then awaited Chris, Tracey and Toby's return later for a very chatty evening meal that seemed to last a very long time.

We hoped we hadn't bored their son and Tracey with our stories, but they both seemed to enjoy themselves and we were glad that we'd managed to meet up with Chris Mill and he'd been part of another day's adventure and with lots of laughs. We wished them goodbye until we'd see them again at Jonny and Jane Martyn's wedding on the Saturday.

Chris and I returned to the room and were starting to get mentally adjusted for our penultimate full day's walking ahead, to re-visit one of our youthful outer reaches of good old Boscastle and the famous Cobweb Inn.

Chapter 14 – Boscastle

The morning of Thursday the 11th July 2013 was another hot sunny one and looked to be heading the same way as the previous day. After my breathless incident yesterday and general tiredness we decided on a split move where Chris was going to walk the coast and I would get the bus to Tintagel. Not ideal but I was a little nervous to head out for yet another hot, no breeze day, this time with my full rucksack, and I think just sheer weariness was setting in and I felt the need for a morning off. We had really not planned enough recovery time and my stamina should have been worked on a lot more before we'd started the adventure, but you only learn your limits when you are at them. The key is listen to your body and don't push it unless there is no alternative. Chris was in agreement too.

However, he was still keen to keep walking and it would mean I could sort the accommodation out and get us a decent spot in a pub for an early lunch, taking it easy on Tintagel beach, whilst he did the Treligga and Trebarwith sands walk and claim moral victory of walking probably 10-15 miles more than me over the whole trip by now.

We had one small final problem before setting out and that was easily overcome. We were nearly 3 miles inland from the footpath but after chatting to the duty manager she arranged for us to get a lift from their Hungarian (see what I mean about all over the world) staff member who was driving into Port Isaac to give us a lift to Port Gaverne on the way, as long as we made a contribution to his petrol, which we did. So swiftly arriving in the village and the bus stop I gave Chris a good luck thumbs up and see you in Tintagel in a few hours.

Arriving fairly quickly by the efficient local bus I took the road straight down to Tintagel beach and the dramatic Merlin's cave dug out on the left hand side. There was no-one around as I was probably two hours ahead of the tourist crowds, so I sat down and took in the peace and beauty of the place texting Chris to say I was good and he texted back the same, yes communications were working down here, thank goodness. It was a very nice recovery for me and after an hour of chilling I made my way into the town and my pub recce picked the "Cornishman Inn" as it was bang on the main road that Chris would come up and had a decent pub garden in the shade at the back too. Plus it served all our favourite beers. I then had enough time to have a look at the Old Post Office and speak to the Boscastle Riverside hotel to confirm our arrival at around 6pm-ish later.

Chris texted his progress was good and he'd be with me between 12-30 and 1pm. It was not long before I saw him trekking along the road and I'd already got his refreshment pint ready as he'd covered the distance really quickly. However, after he sat down took his boots and socks off to let his feet cool down he asked me if the slate stones here were absolutely freezing, as that is was it felt like to him, but they weren't. They were a bit cooler than the surrounding stones/pavement but they were actually warm given the days heat and I was wondering if Chris's foot nerves were suffering from the accumulation of thirteen days solid walking and not working properly. He wasn't convinced but we both agreed that at the Riverside Hotel in Boscastle later we'd make sure the room had a bath and he'd better bathe his feet to give them a good soak and rest them as much as he could. Neither of us wanted to be injured now with the end of the walk coming into view and both us keen to walk into Bude, no buses or taxis, or ambulances, just on our own two feet, especially after all we'd been through up to now.

After that we settled down for a big blow-out two hour monster lunch and another couple of beers as the walk to Boscastle was a nice three to four hour stretch ahead of us and we'd make it comfortably for 6-7pm. The views were again superb and the weather held out all the way and it was nice as for the first time in a while as it was just the two of us once more out on the coast. We both reflected that it had seemed an age since the two of us had set out towards East Portholland thirteen days before on the south coast with no idea how it would go with just a cheerful hope it would all be ok.

The path and the cliffs weave in and out here rather than undulate, so there were lots of overhangs and steep cliff drops with great views. Here was where we managed to get our front cover iconic picture shot of Chris's walking boots hanging by the edge, with the sea and cliff view of the Cornish coast falling back in the distance.

After a few water breaks and generally easy walking for us we were soon through rocky valley and were making our way towards Boscastle comfortably, and I wasn't struggling at all today, well I shouldn't have after the morning off I hear you cry!

We came in by the harbour entrance and passed Warren Point and made our way up into the town itself noting the newish stonework, new bridge and general repairs that's were obvious from the old buildings after the terrible flash flood of August 2004. We found the Riverside Hotel and it was definitely a higher calibre of accommodation, but we'd planned it that way as it was our last night away on the walk. It was also going to be the two of us heading to the Cobweb Inn for a quiet meal but Chris got a text from Adrian and his family as they wanted to come down and visit again. It was one of those we'd almost have preferred to have a quiet evening to ourselves after so much hosting, but Adrian was very keen to come down and chat. He is also sadly not with us anymore as he died last year in 2017 and had suffered from Polio all his life, yes it is still there as a disease and anyone who says the vaccine is too dangerous should see what Polio does to you, my Uncle had suffered from it too all his life, it's not pleasant I can assure you. We also needed his eighteen year old son to get us Wi-Fi connected in two minutes instead of two hours, just like he'd done at St Agnes earlier in the trip, so it was a bonus having them back again. There was a few extra things we needed to do on the social media front as tomorrow we would be on the last day home to Bude and we needed to get the message out.

A pleasant evening was had with us reminiscing of stolen nights down here with various car drivers learning their trade at seventeen or eighteen, bombing down the A and B roads from Bude and Kilkhampton with too many people in the car, piling into the Cobweb Inn for beers and then tearing back to Bude or Widemouth Manor for the nightclub all in the same night. The things you do when you are that young, fit and able to function without sleep… talking of which we needed some and Chris was a bit concerned about his feet after the day's events, so we bade them a fond farewell and headed back to the luxurious room where we had baths to soak our feet and limbs and get packed for the last full day of walking. Our excitement level was high as we thought about tomorrow's homecoming final trek.

Chapter 15 - Bude

Friday the 12th July 2013 was another good weather day and dawned as bright as all the others, so a good omen for the final walk to Bude. Outside the river (hence the name of the hotel) was flowing freely and providing a very relaxing background noise as it bubbled passed our window below. Talking of being relaxed and feeling the effects of the long walk we agreed over breakfast that we'd catch the bus to Crackington Haven and walk from there to Bude. We were in demob happy mode and knowing that Chris had an evening meal/big family celebration planned for his homecoming later. I was meeting an old friend from my youth who was in Bude at the same time with her family, so we couldn't afford to be slow. We thought if we front loaded the day like this we would not mess up everyone else's plans by arriving late, tired, injured and weary after another long day in the heat. Well that's our story and we're sticking to it.

So after settling up the bill we saw all the tourists arriving by the coachloads to cram into the town and sat by the bridge over the river Valency. After a short wait chatting and avoiding the droves of tourists heading down into the harbour, it wasn't long before we were transported on the bus via the B3263 to Crackington Haven, and the first walk of the day, up the massive angled hill beside the inlet. It really felt here like the home run as we'd spent more time than we care to remember around this inlet and the Coombe Barton Inn and beach over our youth, it still looked the same but felt different at the same time, odd somehow.

Anyway we were anticipating a tough walk to Millhook, which was 4.5 miles away and from our road knowledge the hill there was a one in three or 33%, depending what sign was now up. As we started the texts had been arriving. My older brother Pete, saying he'd like to join us at some point for the walk to Bude so gave him the rough plan and where we thought we'd be. My oldest friend Rob Simpson (who lived next door and I'd known since I was four years old) was not so keen for the walk but texting he was happy to meet me and/or Chris for a beer later. Tim and Finlay the dog would re-join us for beers too so a local gathering of the clans was developing. My friend Johanna Groon-Lim was keen to sort out the evening arrangements, with two sons in tow, and looking forward to meeting up at the Brendon Arms with everyone. It would be the first time we'd met up since we were eighteen but more of that story later. Chris too was getting his family information and plans sorted and had agreed to meet them on the beach after the walk and then they'd be off for their evening celebration.

We had one very difficult area to negotiate before we even came to Millhook, which we thought would be the tough one. It turns out that a rising slope just passed St Gennys on the way to the Dizzard was in fact a rock climb. Our friend Tim had mentioned something about this way back in Portreath, but we hadn't understood what he meant until now. At one point as I climbed up using both my hands for grip and balance, I looked up and Chris appeared to be vertically above my left shoulder doing the same thing. We needed a water and breath break at the top of that and we'd been worrying about Millhook! The reality of the coastal path compared to the road was in fact fairly easy and we managed it with a lot less hassle than we thought possible, as we reminisced about cycling and driving (or being driven, probably to the Coombe Barton Inn) up and down the dreaded coast road over the years.

Another text from my brother trying to find us he was having trouble working out where we were. He had no idea how fast you can cover ground and in the end agreed to meet us at Widemouth bay and walk the last few miles with us. I think he wanted to do more but we'd already gone passed where he thought we were and had to settle for that.

It felt even odder as we came through the next headland and could see Widemouth bay, Lundy Island and the straightish coastline all the way to Bude itself. Descending down to walk the length of the beach on the sand at Widemouth, which where the coastal path is to avoid the busy coast road, my older brother was no-where to be seen. We had to do a bit of back tracking and a quick call and he emerged by the sand dunes as he'd had trouble parking the car due to the busy atmosphere of a holiday Friday down here and had missed us again. He looked well and we went through the family chat and he was amazed at the pace of how fast we walked, which of course we couldn't tell but I'm sure it was the homecoming factor that spurred us on.

Having him there helped a lot with the photos too, as we didn't have to bother any tourists to get the iconic shots of the final bit of the walk. We passed the dunes and downs at Efford and could see the breakwater of Summerleaze beach ahead of us and the town nestled into the surrounding countryside, to the right, our hometown. We both had a few silent moments thinking to ourselves as we traversed the slope up to Compass point. Stopping at the top of the big hill overlooking the town for a few photo shots and to take it all in, and then we simply plodded down the hill and into the final part of the walk, the Canal towpath and Lock Gate Bridge where we agreed the finishing line would be. The sun was beaming down and Pete took the last official photo of me and Chris shaking hands at the lock gates where the walk was finally ended after some 200-220 miles. What a journey indeed.

We said our goodbyes at the lock gate as Chris headed off in the other direction via the bridge and Summerleaze beach to meet his family, whilst Pete and I walked along the breakwater road to the Brendon Arms for a well-earned pint, by the canal and passed where we once had lived in the late 1960's. Our gran was even born in this road in 1882, so an historic place for the family.

After this we had a very pleasant late afternoon/evening meet up with Rob, Tim, and Finlay the dog and my friend Johanna and her 2 sons. She was a Swedish language student when I first met her when we were eighteen, and we'd been good friends then, but as you do you lose touch over time as there was no e-mail, Facebook, Snapchat, WhatsApp, and Instagram back then, only expensive phone calls or letters. We'd written a few times, but your life moves on and the contact disappears, or did. However, a mutual friend at the time Anna Nyman, who was in Bude as a language student with us in 1980 found me on Facebook a few years before the trip, looking up another Bude school friend who'd moved to Australia. So we rekindled the contact after a gap of nearly thirty years online, exactly what social media is for. She had always loved Bude and England, and comes back whenever she can with her family and managed to coincide her trip with our epic journey. I thought it would be very strange to meet up after thirty two years, but it wasn't at all. Physically we hadn't changed that much either. We'd both got life experience by the bucket loads to share in the chat, but we were still those eighteen years olds looking at life, deep down aren't we all really? Rob was on great form too in his usual chatty way and it was good to see him and always feels like home with him around. Tim was keen to catch up too from where we'd left him Portreath and was on form as well with Finlay adding to the fun by stealing someone's food at the next table too. Before we knew it was time for everyone to leave and me to head home and my sister-in-law Jill to kindly give me a lift, saving me from another walk with a big rucksack after an emotional day. A good way to finish.

THE END JOURNEY AND CONCLUDING NOTES

Chris and I met up again the following day for our friend's wedding in a field tent, on a farm, on a hill in glorious sunshine, fabulous and a chance to talk about the trip to our friends and without a rucksack in sight. He had had a great evening with his family the night before but said it was odd not having his wing-man there with the kitty for beer and food, and not having his rucksack either.

To finally get back to our lives in the South East we travelled on the Sunday via the local bus from Bude to Exeter and then the train to Reading and London, which was so packed from returning holiday makers we couldn't get a seat together so the passengers were spared the "where are we train app chat" of the downward journey. So it was a quiet reflective few hours of travel. A chance to gather our own thoughts of the whole trip and re-charge a bit before home. The train ride together ended when Chris got off at Reading for his home return and I continued onto London Paddington station then via the tube and Thameslink train to my home in Harpenden. The funny thing was that earlier on the Sunday morning both of us felt we had to walk from our respective brother and sister houses in Bude to the bus stop in town, both done independently of each other with our rucksacks fully packed and no offer of a lift or taxi was to be accepted. We both felt we needed to walk again and if we could have the time off and money we'd just keep going and walk as far as John O'Groats and back, to be done one day in the future… maybe.

In terms of general fitness I think once the feet had toughened up and with the right rest and adaption to weather conditions, we could have kept going almost indefinitely. I certainly haven't felt as fit as after the walk and Chris proved his stamina training paid off big time over the two weeks. We both weighed ourselves before we started and when we got home and we were almost exactly the same weight. My wife thought I'd lost weight and Chris's partner thought he'd lost weight too, but it was all about shape change. The stomach muscles had gone in, the back, shoulder and chest muscles out to support the rucksack carrying, and our legs did the rest. Thus proving our hypothesis that whatever and however much we drank or ate we could walk it off, and shape up at the same time too.

We hope we have encouraged you, through our adventures, to get your rucksack out from the garage, cupboard, wardrobe, attic or bin and dust off your walking boots/shoes/trainers and just go exploring. The pub side of things may not be for you, and we do understand that, however pubs are the main places you'll find out on your walks especially in the country, for food, rest and even accommodation and the catering for all tastes went well beyond our expectations, so we hope you find that too.

Just start planning your own trip of what you hope you can and want to achieve, however big or small. You never know who you will meet along the way, you can't plan exactly what will happen, which is good for your fun level, and it's very good for your overall health, especially cognitive functioning (I made that bit up) and of course its character building too. The adventures just happen as you go along as I hope we have shown. It's also preferable to share with a good friend or two as we are confident you will enjoy one of the best and simplest things in life, walking.

Chris and Mike – July 2018

APPENDIX

1. Guide and Map Book:
   The Trailblazer Guide, published July 2012
   Cornish Coast Path – South West Coast Path Part 2 - Bude to Plymouth

2. Accommodation Details:

2013	**Destination**	**Accommodation**
Saturday 29th June	East Portholland	Tubbs Mill House - 01872 531852
Sunday 30th	Falmouth	Braemar Guest House - 01326 311285
Monday 1st July	Coverack	Penmarth House - 01326 280240
Tuesday 2nd	Mullion	Mounts Bay B&B - 01326 241761
Wednesday 3rd	Marazion	Netherleigh B&B - Now Closed
Thursday 4th	Porthcurno	Sea View House - 01736 810638
Friday 5th	St Ives	Atlantic Hotel - 01736 796177
Saturday 6th	Portreath	Dolphin House - Now Closed
Sunday 7th	St Agnes	St Agnes Hotel - 01872 552307
Monday 8th	Crantock	Garden Cottage - 01637 830806
Tuesday 9th	Padstow	The Harlyn Inn - 01841 520207
Wednesday 10th	Port Isaac	Cornish Arms - 01208 880263
Thursday 11th	Boscastle	Riverside Hotel - 01840 250216
Friday 12th	Bude	Family Homes

3. Facebook Page Link
   https://www.facebook.com/CornishFootpathWalk2013/

www.ingramcontent.com/pod-product-compliance
Ingram Content Group UK Ltd.
Pitfield, Milton Keynes, MK11 3LW, UK
UKHW041844200726
13854UKWH00005BA/2068

9 781789 555042